THE NATH RELIGION

The Incredible Naths and Shri Dattatreya

RAGHUPATI BHATT

978-1-7638613-3-6

THE NATH RELIGION:
THE INCREDIBLE NATHS AND SHRI DATTATREYA
Raghupati Bhatt

MANTICORE PRESS
WWW.MANTICORE.PRESS

CONTENTS

FOREWORD..5

THE NATH RELIGION 9

AADINATH 17

SHRI DATTATREYA 27

SHRIPAD SHRI VALLABH 37

SHRI NARASIMHA SARASWATI 39

SHRI GURU'S ADVICE...43

SHRI SWAMI SAMARTH..47

SHRI MANIK PRABHU 51

SHRI SAIBABA..57

MACHHINDRANATH 63

GORAKSHANATH OR GORARKHNATH............................73

GAHININATH..81

JALANDARNATH..87

KANIF NATH 91

BHARTRUHARINATH...97

CHARPATNATH..101

CHOURANGI NATH..105

NAGNATH 107

REVAN NATH 109

ADBANGINATH...115

THE NATH TRADITION 119

THE INFLUENCE OF THE NATH CULT............................123

SOME UNKNOWN TALES OF THE NATH CULT 127

GORAKHNATH'S BOOKS 139

GORAKSHPADDHATI..141

DNYANESHWARI ON KUNDALINI 149

THE BHAKTI SAMPRADAYA...155

FORWARD

This is an account of the Nath religion. I first learned about the Naths in school when our teacher, Shri Bapusaheb Raut, introduced them to us. He had been on a pilgrimage to North India and shared his knowledge about the Nath Yogis.

There are numerous narratives regarding the Nathpanthis. Several sacred texts have been written about them, and various saints have documented their insights on this group.

There are nine prominent personalities, along with many others who are equally powerful as the main Gurus.

All of them achieved Samadhi. They concluded their lives by either retreating into caves or disappearing without explanation.

Some believe that prominent Naths are immortal, appearing to devotees centuries later.

It is a question of faith.

They include members from all Hindu castes and also feature some Muslim shrines.

It is believed by some that there are eminent sages residing in the caves of the Himalayas.

The renowned Vedic seers also resided in the snow-covered caves.

We call them Saptarishis.

In Nath tradition, the pilgrimage to Badrikashrama is

essential. This site houses a temple dedicated to Vishnu. I've heard that many sages are performing penance in Himalayan caves, but their ages are unknown.

During the recent Kumbha Mela, several of these Sadhus attended.

According to Shri Ramkrishna, powerful sadhus are present around you, but you cannot see them unless they choose to reveal themselves.

One may seek the blessings of Nath Gurus. The phrase they say is "Allakh Niranjan." It is challenging to identify genuine Sadhus.

Some individuals once asked Shri Ramkrishna, "Where can we find an accomplished Sadhu?"

Shri Ramkrishna indicated a man dressed in tattered clothing, who was sitting among stray dogs and consuming discarded food.

He fled when approached and was never seen again.

The Naths have established several mathas, which possess chronological records tracing their origins.

Herein are the remarkable accounts of the notable Nath personalities.

They do not have any geographical boundaries. They could also be in Europe or America.

If one is fortunate, he or she may encounter them. This luck is associated with Karma.

Happy reading and best of luck.

I am thankful to all the sages who wrote down the accounts of the Naths.

I would like to express my profound gratitude to the Gurus who have bestowed upon me some of the most remarkable stories.

I am indebted to Gwendolyn Taunton and her editorial team of Manticore.

This is my fourth book with Gwendolyn.

I dedicate this book to my wife Vijaya.
Allakh Niranjan.
I pray to the formless, pure and
transcendent Ultimate Truth.
Bless us all.

THE NATH RELIGION

The Nath Yogis belong to the Hindu religion and possess distinct characteristics that set them apart. Their practices are known to be rigorous and demanding, adhering to strict rules and pathways that are often considered challenging to follow. These paths are metaphorically described as slippery, requiring immense discipline and dedication. Even the supposed founder of the Nath cult, Machhindranath, is said to have deviated from the prescribed path for a certain period.

The origins of the Nath tradition are commonly attributed to Aadinath; a title often associated with Shiva. Shiva is revered as the primordial teacher and the spiritual guide of this cult. The Nath tradition is rich with fascinating stories and legends; each Nath being associated with extraordinary tales that enhance the mystique surrounding them. Among the Naths, nine are considered particularly prominent, referred to as the Navanaths. However, in addition to these nine, there are others whose contributions and teachings are also recognized.

Numerous texts and scriptures have been written about the Naths, each offering a wealth of information and insights into their lives, philosophies, and practices. These writings delve deep into the spiritual and practical aspects of the Nath tradition, providing a comprehensive view of their methods to achieve self-realization and enlightenment. The

Nath cult represents a profound spiritual lineage intertwined with Hinduism, reflecting the diversity and depth of Indian spiritual traditions.

The concept of the Navanaths forms a central aspect of the Nath tradition, yet variations in the lists of these nine Naths are observed across different sources. One list notably omits Gorakshanath, an omission that is striking considering his foundational role in shaping the Nath tradition. Gorakshanath is revered as a pivotal figure, often regarded as the progenitor of the practices and philosophies that define this spiritual lineage.

The origins of the Nath tradition are deeply intertwined with Shiva, also known as Shankar, who is considered the initiator of this profound spiritual path. Within Indian spirituality, various cults have emerged, each reflecting unique dimensions of the quest for self-realization. Prominent among these are the Shaivite tradition, the Vaishnavite tradition, and Shaktism. These cults embody distinct theological frameworks and practices, yet they are unified by their ultimate goal of spiritual enlightenment.

In later developments, the Ganapati tradition emerged as an influential spiritual path within Hinduism. Followers of this tradition are often referred to as Ganapatyas. This tradition further emphasizes the diversity and richness of Indian spiritual heritage, showcasing the multiplicity of approaches to achieving the singular goal of self-realization and universal connection. Such interconnectedness underscores the philosophical depth of Indian spirituality, where distinct paths converge to reflect the unity within diversity.

The later development of the Datta cult attempted to unify various spiritual traditions under one overarching framework. Dattatreya, a revered figure in Indian spirituality, embodies the combined qualities of Brahma, Vishnu, and

Shiva, symbolizing the harmonious integration of diverse traditions. Scholars have often noted connections between the Nath tradition and the Datta cult, suggesting a shared philosophical lineage that emphasizes the pursuit of self-realization. This pursuit is a central theme across myriad spiritual paths, each offering unique approaches to attain the ultimate goal.

A Sanskrit verse beautifully encapsulates this unity of spiritual paths:

Akashat patitam toyam yatha gachchati sagaram|
Sarva dev namaskaram Keshavam pratigachchati||

Translated, it means: "As all water falling from the sky reaches the sea, salutations to all deities ultimately reach Keshava." This verse highlights the profound idea that all spiritual endeavors lead to the same ultimate truth.

Some scholars speculate that the origins of the Nath tradition may lie in the Shakta practices. These practitioners, particularly in the early stages, were believed to follow the Vamachara path, a Tantric tradition characterized by unconventional and esoteric rituals. The term Vamachara, derived from the Sanskrit word Vama (left), refers to the "left-hand path" in Tantric practices, which were often controversial for their inclusion of taboo elements.

Vamachara adherents followed what are often referred to as the 'Five M's,' which include:

- Madya (wine)
- Mansa (meat)
- Maithuna (sexual intercourse)
- Matsya (fish)
- Mudra (grain)

These practices involved consuming meat and fish, drinking wine, engaging in sexual rituals, and performing symbolic gestures associated with yoga. The Vamachara tradition viewed these activities as mediums to transcend worldly attachments and achieve spiritual salvation or Mukti.

This approach, while unconventional, was founded on the belief that the path to liberation required confronting and overcoming societal and personal inhibitions. Through these symbolic acts, practitioners sought to break free from the limitations of the material world, embracing a state of higher consciousness and ultimate unity with the divine.

Such philosophical diversity underscores the richness of Indian spiritual traditions, where numerous paths converge toward the shared goal of enlightenment and universal truth. This interconnectedness exemplifies the depth and adaptability of Indian spirituality, reflecting the seamless blend of unity within diversity.

In spiritual practices, sexual activity has historically been recognized as a potent source of pleasure, second only to the profound bliss experienced in Samadhi, the ultimate state of spiritual realization. However, such indulgence is fraught with risks, particularly the danger of becoming fixated on physical gratification at the expense of spiritual growth and enlightenment. This delicate balance between worldly pleasure and transcendental aspiration is a theme deeply woven into the narratives of the Nath tradition.

The stories within the Nath tradition often highlight this tension, particularly those centered around Matsyendranath, the revered first Nath. Matsyendranath is frequently depicted as both embodying and transcending earthly desires in his spiritual journey, illustrating the profound challenges and rewards associated with navigating the path of Tantric practices. His life serves as a testament to the complexities inherent in using worldly experiences as vehicles for spiritual elevation, a concept that resonates through the rich tapestry of Tantric philosophy.

Through these narratives, the Nath tradition offers valuable insights into the interplay between indulgence and discipline, reminding practitioners to remain vigilant and resolute in their pursuit of divine connection while acknowledging the transformative potential of confronting human desires. These teachings underscore the broader philosophical framework of Indian spirituality, where the convergence of personal experience and universal truth leads to the ultimate goal of enlightenment.

Aadinath, commonly identified as Shiva, is venerated in his iconic phallic representation, known as the Shiva Linga. This symbol embodies the creative and destructive powers of the universe, highlighting the cyclical nature of existence. Festivals such as Maha Shivaratri celebrate Shiva's divine essence, during which devotees partake in consuming bhang, an intoxicant prepared from cannabis leaves, as an offering and act of devotion.

Female Vamacharies, practitioners of the left-handed Tantric path, also played a significant role in the spiritual landscape of ancient India. These female ascetics often engaged in philosophical and ritualistic confrontations with the Naths, showcasing the dynamic interplay between differing spiritual ideologies. Their presence and practices were not confined to specific regions but extended across the entirety of the Indian subcontinent, marking a profound cultural and philosophical impact.

The roaming nature of these women Vamacharies allowed them to influence diverse communities, leaving traces of their unique spiritual approach in various corners of the country. Their legacy persists in the form of stories, rituals, and traditions that celebrate the multifaceted nature of Indian spirituality.

The traditions of women Tantriks, particularly those residing in Kamroopa (modern-day Assam), played a significant role in shaping the Tantric practices of ancient India. Kamroopa, renowned for its spiritual heritage, was home to the revered Kamakhya temple, which served as the central pilgrimage site for these practitioners of Shakta Tantra.

The rituals and offerings conducted at the Kamakhya temple were deeply symbolic and ritualistic, reflecting the profound connection between the material and spiritual realms. Sacrificial offerings, including animals, were made to the Goddess Kamakhya as acts of devotion and as representations of the transformative energies inherent in the cycle of creation and destruction. In addition to these offerings, wine was also presented to the deity, symbolizing purity and the freeing of spiritual inhibitions.

The practices followed by these Tantriks underscored the vast diversity within Indian spirituality, presenting a striking contrast to the more ascetic traditions of the Naths. Their influence extended beyond the boundaries of Kamroopa, leaving an indelible mark on the cultural and spiritual fabric of the Indian subcontinent.

The reverence and practices observed by the devotees were imbued with deep symbolism and devotion, reflecting the intricate tapestry of spiritual traditions within the region. However, the transformative shift in the Nath sect's trajectory occurred under the stewardship of Gorakshanath, or Gorakh-Nath, who is widely regarded as the pivotal figure and true architect of the Nath cult.

Gorakshanath's contributions elevated the cult from its earlier associations with Shaktas and Vamacharis, steering it toward a path of greater theological and philosophical cohesion. His profound influence laid the foundation for the sect's expansion and its enduring legacy within the spiritual framework of Indian subcontinental traditions. Further exploration of Gorakshanath's role and his teachings will be elaborated in a dedicated section discussing his impact and significance.

AADINATH

Adi, meaning "beginning," signifies the origins of the Nath cult, which is traditionally attributed to Shri Shankar, a figure known by many revered names. In the Vedic texts, he is referred to as Rudra, while later traditions came to recognize him as Shiva, the great ascetic and cosmic destroyer. Together with Brahma and Vishnu, Shiva forms the trinity of divinity central to the Hindu cosmological worldview. Brahma, as the creator, initiates the cycles of existence, Vishnu sustains and nurtures the universe, and Shiva presides over its ultimate dissolution, paving the way for regeneration. This cyclical process is believed to be eternal and foundational to the dynamics of creation.

Within this broader spiritual framework, two prominent sects emerged: Vaishnavism, devoted to Vishnu, and Shaivism or Smarta sects, centered around the worship of Shiva. Despite their shared roots in Hindu philosophy, the followers of these two sects often found themselves in rivalry, each asserting the supremacy of their chosen deity. Numerous mythological narratives were conceived to substantiate claims of divine precedence, illustrating the rich tapestry of theological debate within the tradition.

These stories not only served to bolster devotional fervor but also shaped the cultural and spiritual ethos of the communities involved. Over time, efforts were made to reconcile these divisions, fostering unity among the sects and emphasizing the interconnectedness of their respective beliefs. The Nath cult itself symbolizes this synthesis, as it integrates diverse elements from Shaivism, Vaishnavism, and other spiritual traditions, creating a holistic framework that transcends sectarian boundaries.

Efforts toward unity among diverse spiritual traditions have been evident throughout history, particularly in the formation of the Datta cult. This cult venerates Lord Dattatreya, who is depicted with three heads symbolizing the combined essence of Brahma, Vishnu, and Shiva. Such symbolism represents the unity of the creative, nurturing, and destructive forces within the universe. Interestingly, Brahma, despite his integral role in creation, is seldom worshipped; there are only a few temples dedicated to him, including one situated in the village of Brahma Karmali in Goa.

The Datta cult serves as a bridge between the major sects of Shaivism and Vaishnavism, fostering a synthesis that underscores the interconnectedness of these traditions. Aadinath, also known as Shankara or Mahadeva, is acknowledged as the initiator of this integration. Mahadeva is further revered by the Lingayat or Veerashaiva communities, who worship Shiva in the form of the Linga. The Linga itself is a profound symbolic representation of fertility, embodying both Shiva and Shakti in their complementary aspects. This duality highlights the significance of balance and unity within the cosmic framework.

Shiva's abode, Mount Kailash, holds immense spiritual significance and is located in Tibet, now part of China. Alongside Mount Kailash lies Lake Mansarovar, a sacred site for followers of various faiths, including Hinduism, Buddhism, Jainism. Pilgrimage to these holy places requires formal permission from the Chinese government, adding an element of exclusivity to their spiritual pursuit.

The sanctity of Mount Kailash is further emphasized by its profound connection to Lord Shiva, who is believed to reside there with his consort Parvati and their two sons, Kartikeya and Ganapati. The mountain itself remains unscaled, as mountaineering is strictly prohibited, preserving its divine and untouchable essence. Even aerial routes above this region are restricted, reinforcing the reverence accorded to this sacred space.

Mount Kailash is revered as the divine abode. This prohibition ensures that the mountain retains its untouchable and transcendent essence, maintaining its status as an unspoiled sanctuary of divine presence.

Lake Mansarovar is also a sacred site; notable rivers like Sindhu or Indus, Sutlej, and the mighty Brahmaputra originate from Mansarovar. It also represents the mind.

According to tradition, Lord Shiva resides on Mount Kailash alongside his consort, Goddess Parvati, and their two sons, Kartikeya and Ganapati. The mountain, enveloped in mysticism and mythological significance, has been a focal point of spiritual reverence across multiple faiths, including Hinduism, Buddhism and Jainism.

Several Puranic scriptures are dedicated to Shiva, offering profound insights into his attributes and deeds. It is widely believed that Shiva predates the Vedic era and shares notable similarities with the Vedic deity Rudra. Through centuries of spiritual evolution, Shiva became Mahadeva— the Great God—adored and venerated as the embodiment of cosmic balance and transcendence.

One of Shiva's most distinctive features is his fair complexion contrasted by the striking blue hue of his throat—a mark of his extraordinary act during the legendary churning of the ocean. As the Devas and Asuras churned the ocean in search of divine treasures, a bowl of poison emerged among the fourteen jewels. None dared to consume it, fearing its destructive potency. To save the universe, Lord Shiva drank the poison, which remained lodged in his throat, turning it blue. This act earned him the epithet "Neelkanth," meaning "the one with the blue throat."

The symbolism of Shiva extends to his physical appearance, where the crescent moon adorning his knotted hair represents the passage of time, and the river Ganga flowing from his locks signifies the purification and sustenance of life. His body, covered in ash, denotes the impermanence of material existence, while the snakes encircling him embody the cycle of life and death, aspects he transcends through eternal meditation and cosmic balance. Thus, Shiva's abode and his mythological persona inspire profound reverence, serving as an enduring symbol of unity, spirituality, and the cosmic order.

There are many stories woven around Shiva. All of them highlight the benevolent nature of this great God. Whenever his devotees practised penance and asked for a boon, he granted them whatever they requested. Sometimes this caused problems, and Vishnu had to devise a plan to resolve them.

After the Great Mother Goddess, or alongside her, Shiva was worshipped. There, incarnations of Vishnu, Shri Ram, and Shri Krishna were devoted followers of Shiva.

As a deity of cosmic balance, Shiva is often depicted in deep meditation, transcending the material realm and embodying profound serenity and spiritual enlightenment.

His selfless act of consuming the poison serves as a timeless symbol of his role as the protector of creation, affirming his status as both the savior and the eternal mediator who unifies the forces of the cosmos.

Adorned with serpents draped across his form and enveloped in ash, Lord Shiva embodies an awe-inspiring presence, both formidable and serene. His hair, tied meticulously in a knot, bears the gentle glow of a crescent moon nestled within, symbolizing the cyclical nature of time and cosmic balance.

The sacred river Ganga, revered for its purifying and liberating essence, is said to have originated from Shiva himself. One ancient narrative recounts the tale of King Sagara's hundred sons, whose arrogance provoked the wrath of a sage. Consumed by his anger, the sage reduced them to ash, condemning their souls to wander without salvation. To deliver them from their plight, it became essential to summon the divine river Ganga from the heavens to cleanse their souls and grant them eternal peace.

This divine task was not without its challenges. Ganga, descending with immense force and vigor, risked overwhelming the earthly realm with her torrential currents. Only Shiva, the cosmic mediator, possessed the ability to temper her celestial flow. Gathering Ganga within his matted locks, he moderated her descent, ensuring her waters brought liberation without destruction. Thus, Shiva's act became a profound symbol of compassion and balance, bridging the heavens and earth in a harmonious union.

One of the descendants of King Sagara, known as Bhagiratha, is credited with the monumental task of bringing the celestial river Ganga down to Earth, which is why the river is also referred to as Bhagirathi. However, Ganga's descent was marked by a torrential and uncontrollable force, capable of devastating the earthly realm. Only Lord Shiva, with his unparalleled strength and cosmic wisdom, could moderate her flow. Gathering Ganga within his matted locks, Shiva tempered her current, ensuring a gentle yet purposeful descent. This divine intervention not only preserved the sanctity of the earthly plane but also liberated the hundred sons of King Sagara, granting them eternal salvation.

This narrative serves as a profound allegory symbolizing the origins of the sacred river Ganga and its connection to the Himalayas. It also hints at the possibility that the Himalayan region, referred to as "Sagara" in Sanskrit, may have once been submerged under the sea.

Adorned with an array of formidable beings known as ganas, Shiva's presence is both awe-inspiring and enigmatic. Among his sacred instruments is the damru, a small drum with a resonant bass tone that echoes the rhythmic pulse of the cosmos. This instrument embodies the essence of Shiva's role as the creator and orchestrator of universal harmony, resonating with the primal sound from which all existence is said to have emerged.

Shiva, revered as one of the most enigmatic and multifaceted deities of Hindu mythology, is also celebrated as a supreme dancer. His cosmic dance, known as *Tandava*, signifies the cycle of creation and destruction, embodying the rhythm of the universe itself. In this form, Shiva earns the epithet *Nataraja*, the Lord of Dance, symbolizing his role as the originator of all performing arts and the orchestrator of universal harmony.

Another intriguing aspect of Shiva is his manifestation as *Ardhanarishvara*, a form where he is depicted as half male and half female, merging both masculine and feminine energies into a single unified entity. This profound representation underscores the inherent balance of opposites in nature and suggests that every individual possesses both male and female aspects within. Such symbolism extends beyond mythology, offering timeless philosophical insights into human existence and the interconnectedness of all beings.

Shiva is also attributed with the origins of yoga, a practice that harmonizes the mind, body, and spirit. Central to this discipline is the art and science of breathing, detailed extensively in the ancient text *Shiva Swarodaya*. This revered scripture delves into the techniques of controlling one's breath, imparting knowledge that is believed to empower individuals to gain mastery over their bodies and eliminate maladies. It stands as a testament to Shiva's enduring influence on holistic well-being.

Through these myriad aspects, Shiva emerges not merely as a deity but as a profound symbol of the natural world, balance, and the intricate threads connecting existence. His teachings and attributes continue to inspire countless seekers on their spiritual and artistic journeys.

The teachings found within *Shiva Swarodaya* illustrate a profound connection between breath control and mastery over one's physical and mental well-being. This ancient text offers invaluable techniques aimed at harmonizing internal energies, enabling individuals to cleanse their bodies of maladies and attain a state of holistic health. The practice itself reflects Shiva's overarching influence on disciplines that connect the realms of spirituality and physical existence.

Shiva, or Shankara, stands as a figure of immense complexity and depth, embodying myriad facets that seem to transcend traditional divine archetypes. His association with yoga, the balance of masculine and feminine energies in his *Ardhanarishvara* form, and his role as the cosmic dancer intertwine to portray an entity that encapsulates both the rhythm of universal order and the intricacies of human existence. Through his symbolism, the timeless wisdom of nature and interconnectedness emanates, offering guidance to both seekers of spiritual enlightenment and practitioners of artistic expression.

Shiva was united in matrimony with Sati, the devoted daughter of Daksha. However, this union was marred by Daksha's disapproval of his son-in-law, who was perceived as unconventional and ascetic in his lifestyle. Shiva, adorned with ash across his body, clad in deer skin, accompanied by serpents, and dwelling in cremation grounds, did not conform to Daksha's ideals of a suitable match for his daughter.

The discord reached its zenith when Daksha organized a grand *yajna* a sacred fire ritual meant to honor the divine. In a deliberate act of exclusion, he invited all the deities and revered figures, save Shiva. Although Shiva himself remained indifferent to this slight, Sati found the insult to her husband unbearable. Her unwavering loyalty and sense of righteous indignation compelled her to confront Daksha at the ritual. When her appeals to her father failed and she realized the depth of his disdain, Sati chose to immolate herself in the sacrificial flames, an act symbolizing her profound grief and defiance against the insult directed toward Shiva.

This tragic act became a pivotal moment in the cosmic narrative, setting the stage for profound consequences that would resonate across the realm of gods and mortals alike. Overcome with inconsolable grief and unbridled fury, Shiva's anguish knew no bounds upon learning of Sati's demise. His sorrow and rage manifested in a cosmic dance of destruction, threatening the balance of the universe itself. Recognizing the looming peril, Vishnu, the preserver within the Holy Trinity, intervened to restore cosmic equilibrium. In a poignant act of divine resolution, Vishnu wielded his celestial discus, the Sudarshan Chakra, to sever the body of Sati into fifty one pieces. Each fragment descended upon various locations across the Indian subcontinent, sanctifying them as sites of profound spiritual significance.

These fifty one sacred sites, known as Shakti Peethas, became revered centers of worship dedicated to the divine feminine. They symbolize the eternal bond between Shiva and Shakti and serve as focal points for the Mother worshipping cult that venerates the goddess in her myriad manifestations. Each Shakti Peetha is imbued with its unique lore and spiritual aura, drawing devotees from far and wide to honor the essence of primal energy and the union of cosmic forces that sustain the universe.

The Shakti Peethas, as mentioned earlier, hold immense significance within the Nath tradition and broader spiritual practices throughout India. This narrative extends further, revealing the cyclical nature of cosmic relationships and divine reincarnations. Sati, after her tragic self-sacrifice, was reborn as Parvati, the daughter of Himavat, the personification of the Himalayas. Her rebirth was not merely an act of restoration but a divine progression that symbolizes both renewal and persistence in the cosmic order.

Parvati, embodying the essence of Aadishakti—the primordial energy—dedicated herself to austere penance to earn Shiva's affection and eventually succeed in becoming his consort. Their union resonates deeply within Hindu theology, portraying the harmonious convergence of dynamic energy and meditative stillness. Together, Shiva and Parvati symbolize the duality that governs existence—the interplay of creation and destruction, activity and passivity.

Reverence for Shiva and Parvati is exemplified through the countless temples dedicated to them across India. These temples are not merely architectural marvels; they stand as cultural and spiritual landmarks, encapsulating narratives of devotion, renunciation, and cosmic balance. The tales surrounding Parvati, her many names, and the stories linked to each epithet enrich the tapestry of Hindu mythology, offering profound lessons and symbolisms.

As the consort of Shiva, Parvati's role transcends that of a companion; she is the embodiment of Shakti, the life-sustaining force that complements Shiva's ascetic detachment. This divine partnership finds expression in numerous facets of Indian religious practices, art, and literature, perpetuating the enduring legacy of their union and its cosmic significance.

In every depiction of Shiva, he is portrayed as deeply immersed in profound meditation, embodying detachment from the material world and its distractions. His unwavering focus and ascetic existence highlight his transcendence over earthly desires and his commitment to spiritual enlightenment.

This meditative state of Shiva once played a crucial role in a significant mythological event. A demon had been granted a boon that he could only be vanquished by Shiva's offspring. This presented an extraordinary dilemma, as Shiva's perpetual meditation made the prospect of fathering a child seemingly unattainable. To resolve this, the gods appointed the god of love, Kamadeva, with the task of awakening Shiva from his trance. Kamadeva, fully aware of the peril, courageously attempted to disrupt Shiva's meditation by using his divine powers to instill feelings of desire.

However, upon being disturbed, Shiva opened his third eye—a symbol of destruction and cosmic insight—and incinerated Kamadeva instantly. This act not only demonstrated Shiva's immense power but reinforced his persona as the epitome of renunciation, one who is unyielding in his detachment from worldly affairs. Kamadeva's demise led to him being referred to as "Ananga," the bodiless one, and Shiva earned the epithet "Madanant," the destroyer of desire.

SHRI DATTATREYA

Shri Dattatreya holds a revered position within the Nath cult, frequently emerging as a figure of profound spiritual significance and often regarded as the initiator or Guru in the narratives of the sect's practitioners. His life story is enveloped in mystery, marked by an enigmatic chronology that defies precise historical determination.

According to ancient lore, Shri Dattatreya was born to the illustrious sage Atri, one of the Sapta Rishis—the seven great sages of Hindu tradition—and a seer of the Vedas. Atri's wisdom and spiritual stature are deeply woven into the fabric of Hindu mythology, underscoring his influence and importance within the pantheon of sages. His contributions to Vedic literature and spiritual discourse further solidify his legacy as a cornerstone of ancient knowledge and enlightenment.

Dattatreya himself is depicted as a paragon of yogic wisdom and esoteric teachings, serving as a guide and source of inspiration for countless followers across generations. His enigmatic presence and teachings continue to resonate deeply within the philosophical traditions of the Nath cult, embodying a timeless connection to the divine and the pursuit of spiritual liberation.

Atri, the revered sage, and his wife Anusuya resided in their secluded hermitage, enveloped by tranquility and spiritual devotion. It was widely acknowledged that the profound strength of Atri was complemented by the unwavering dedication and virtue of Anusuya. Her unparalleled devotion to her husband elevated their stature, making them a formidable pair in the realm of sages. Such was their divine influence that it was believed they could rival the power of the mighty trinity of deities—Brahma, Vishnu, and Shiva.

The trinity, intrigued by the boundless devotion and spiritual asceticism of Anusuya, resolved to test her virtues and diminish her perceived invincibility. Choosing stealth over confrontation, they descended to her hermitage disguised as humble Brahmins, carefully timing their arrival during Atri's absence. Their intention was clear: to challenge the sanctity of her devotion through deceit and cunning.

Upon their arrival, Anusuya welcomed the guests with grace and hospitality, as was customary in ancient traditions, which provided food to visitors at mealtime was deemed an essential act of piety. Her demeanor reflected the depth of her understanding and her adherence to the highest virtues of dharma. Little did she know that the visitors were none other than the supreme deities, veiled by their mortal guise, intent on testing her unwavering fidelity and moral strength.

Unfolding events soon placed Anusuya's integrity to the test, paving the way for an extraordinary encounter that would redefine the boundaries of devotion and resilience. The three Brahmins appeared weary and famished, their expressions reflecting the toll of their journey. Anusuya, embodying grace and hospitality, addressed them with unwavering kindness, saying, "I shall prepare a wholesome meal for you. Please make yourselves comfortable while I attend to your needs."

One of the Brahmins, however, interjected with a peculiar request. "Respected Mother," he began, his tone measured yet resolute, "We are deeply grateful for your generosity, but we must humbly impose a condition upon this act of kindness. You must serve us the meal unclothed. Should you find this request unacceptable, we shall not linger further and will seek sustenance elsewhere."

Anusuya listened intently, her demeanor unchanged. Her piercing intuition revealed to her that these were no ordinary Brahmins but the supreme deities—Brahma, Vishnu, and Shiva—cloaked in mortal semblance, testing her virtues. Her unwavering composure reflected her profound spiritual strength and wisdom.

She responded with calm assurance, "There is no difficulty in your request. I shall serve you as you wish. I ask only for a moment to prepare your meal." Anusuya proceeded to prepare the food with great care; each act infused with devotion and diligence. Once the meal was ready, she removed her garments, her actions guided by the purity of her intentions and adherence to the highest principles of dharma.

As she stepped outside to serve the food, the scene began to transform into one of divine revelation—a testament to her unparalleled resolve and grace.

Upon stepping outside, Anusuya encountered a profound transformation—the three Brahmins had been replaced by three innocent and radiant infants. Her unwavering virtues had invoked a divine shift, rendering Brahma, Vishnu, and Shiva into their infant forms. This transformation was not merely a display of her spiritual strength but also an affirmation of her unparalleled grace and purity.

The supreme deities had sought to challenge her ideal of wifehood, imposing an extraordinary demand that only her husband could witness her in a state of absolute vulnerability. Yet Anusuya, with her boundless wisdom and unwavering adherence to dharma, transcended their intent.

By transforming them into infants, she upheld the sanctity of her role, for a mother can stand unguarded before her children without compromising her virtue. Such was the extent of Anusuya's spiritual power—a force rooted in her purity and devotion.

When her husband, Atri, returned to the hermitage, his senses were immediately attuned to the divine presence. He heard the soft cries of the infants and found Anusuya nursing them with tender care, embodying the nurturing essence of a divine matriarch. Through his immense psychic insight, Atri discerned the events that had transpired and understood the magnitude of his wife's actions.

However, the absence of Brahma, Vishnu, and Shiva from their cosmic duties began to disrupt the natural order of existence. Creation faltered without Brahma's guidance, preservation weakened without Vishnu's sustenance, and destruction remained unbalanced without Shiva's transformative force. The cosmos awaited resolution, yearning for its equilibrium to be restored.

Brahma is entrusted with the responsibility of creation, Vishnu with preservation and nourishment, and Shiva with the transformative act of destruction. These roles are essential to maintaining the cosmic balance and order within the universe.

When the divine consorts arrived at the hermitage in search of their husbands, they were astonished to find Brahma, Vishnu, and Shiva transformed into helpless infants. This unexpected sight revealed the profound spiritual power and unwavering virtue of Anusuya, who had safeguarded the sanctity of her dharma through her extraordinary actions.

The consorts, deeply concerned about the disruption caused by the absence of their husbands from their divine duties, pleaded with Anusuya to release the deities from their infant forms. Anusuya, understanding the critical need for cosmic harmony, acceded to their request. With her boundless compassion and spiritual wisdom, she restored Brahma, Vishnu, and Shiva to their original divine forms, allowing them to return to their celestial abodes and resume their pivotal roles in the cosmos.

However, the transformation left behind three extraordinary manifestations—Durvasa, Shri Dattatreya, and Chandra, the moon—each imbued with aspects of the celestial triad. These divine offspring were destined to carry forward their unique legacies, bridging the realms of mortals and gods, and further enriching the mythological tapestry of existence.

Durvasa, renowned for his asceticism and divine temperament, sought solitude in the Himalayas to undertake rigorous penance, cultivating his spiritual prowess and connection to the cosmic forces. Chandra, the moon deity, ascended to his celestial position, illuminating the night skies and fulfilling his ordained role in maintaining the harmony of nature.

Shri Dattatreya, imbued with unparalleled wisdom and divinity, remained with his parents, Atri and Anusuya, to uphold their legacy and continue on the path of enlightenment. The name "Dattatreya" holds profound significance: Datta, meaning "given," symbolizes his divine origin, while Atreya, denoting "of Atri," emphasizes his lineage and connection to the revered sage. Thus, the appellation encapsulates both his celestial heritage and his earthly ties. While these accounts are deeply entrenched in the mythological traditions of India, they serve as an enduring testament to the intricate interplay between the mortal and divine realms, inspiring believers to explore the profound mysteries of existence and the timeless narratives of spiritual transcendence.

Atri, his wife Anusuya, and their son Dattatreya may have endeavored to foster unity between the Shaktas and Vaishnavas, two prominent sects that were often engaged in theological debates and conflicts over the supremacy of their respective deities. The Shaktas and other Shaiva sects revered Shiva as the ultimate divine figure, whereas the Vaishnavas held Vishnu as the embodiment of supreme divinity.

Dattatreya, with his profound spiritual wisdom and transcendent presence, emerged as a unifying figure in this divide. Within the Datta Sampradaya and Natha Sampradaya, these sects found common ground, where both Shiva and Vishnu were regarded as integral aspects of the divine. Dattatreya's teachings and actions exemplified a philosophy that transcended sectarian boundaries, advocating for harmony and mutual respect among all devotees.

Dattatreya traversed the length and breadth of India, spreading messages of universal spirituality and seeking to dissolve the animosity between Shaivas and Vaishnavas. His tireless efforts not only contributed to the spiritual enrichment of countless individuals but also paved the way for a more inclusive understanding of divinity, wherein the essence of Shiva and Vishnu could be celebrated together rather than in opposition.

Dattatreya is venerated as an immortal spiritual figure whose teachings have profoundly influenced Indian philosophy and spirituality. Scattered across India, numerous temples are dedicated to him, attesting to his enduring legacy. In artistic representations, Dattatreya is often depicted with three heads and six hands, symbolizing his mastery over creation, preservation, and destruction, as well as his transcendence beyond sectarian boundaries. However, in certain temples and Mutts, he is worshipped as a single-headed figure, emphasizing his unified essence.

Mount Giranar in Gujarat is particularly significant in the Datta tradition, as it houses a revered temple on its summit dedicated to Dattatreya. This sacred site is considered a place of immense spiritual power and is visited by countless devotees seeking enlightenment and solace. The followers of the Datta cult cherish the belief that some individuals embody aspects of Shri Dattatreya, further extending his divine presence among humanity.

Dattatreya's birth is surrounded by numerous incredible tales, all of which converge on the agreement that he was the son of the sage Atri and his devoted wife Anusuya. His life and deeds are extensively chronicled in various Puranas, highlighting his role as a spiritual guide and symbol of harmony. Each narrative adds depth to his persona, portraying him as the bridge between conflicting ideologies and the harbinger of universal spiritual wisdom. His teachings not only resonate with seekers but also serve as a foundation for philosophical texts and practices within the broader Indian spiritual landscape. Through these narratives and his timeless wisdom, Dattatreya continues to inspire generations, fostering an understanding of divinity that transcends sectarian divides and embraces the unity of all existence.

Dattatreya is also credited with composing the revered text known as the *Avadhut Gita*, a profound philosophical discourse that elucidates the nature of reality and the path to spiritual liberation. His teachings have inspired numerous disciples, among whom Sahastrarjuna, also referred to as Kartavirya Arjuna, holds a significant place. Interestingly, Kartavirya's arch-nemesis, Parashurama, was also a devout follower of Dattatreya, highlighting the saint's ability to transcend personal conflicts and unite diverse individuals under the umbrella of his spiritual guidance.

According to tradition, Dattatreya himself sought wisdom from twenty-four gurus, an extraordinary aspect of his life that emphasizes his humility and recognition of the inherent value in all forms of existence. These gurus were not conventional teachers but elements and beings from Mother Nature, each imparting unique lessons that shaped Dattatreya's understanding of the world. This symbolic learning underscores the interconnectedness of life and the profound wisdom embedded in the natural world, offering timeless insights to those on a spiritual quest.

> From Earth, he learnt endurance and peace. From Wind, he learnt the freedom and free flow From Sky, he learnt unlimitedness.

> From Water he learnt indiscrimination. From Fire, he learnt purification.

> From Moon (who was also his brother), he learnt that one's nature remains the same despite the different and difficult times.

> From the Sun, he learnt light and sharing. Pigeons taught him detachment.

> Pythons taught him contentment.

In this way, there are fifteen more like bumblebee, beekeeper, hawk, ocean, moth, elephant, deer, fish, courtesan, child, maiden, snake, Arrowsmith, spider, and, finally, caterpillar.

Shri Guru Dattatreya serves as an eternal beacon of wisdom, a profound teacher who discovered enlightenment through nature and its myriad elements. His teachings are exceptionally unique, as he drew wisdom from seemingly humble and ordinary aspects of the world, recognizing divinity in both animate and inanimate beings. These teachings emphasize harmony with nature and a deep understanding of universal truths.

Dattatreya's philosophy transcends the conventional framework of spirituality. By embracing the lessons from diverse natural entities, he demonstrated that learning is an endless process, available to all who are willing to observe and reflect. This approach firmly establishes him as an environmentalist ahead of his time, one who perceived the interconnectedness of all life forms and the spiritual essence inherent within them.

Moreover, the Datta Sampradaya regards Shri Guru as a timeless presence, embodying the principle of immortality. The belief in his partial incarnations highlights his omnipresence and the continuation of his teachings through various forms and eras. Each incarnation is seen as a manifestation of his enduring spirit, guiding humanity toward enlightenment and unity with the cosmos.

Among these incarnations, notable figures have emerged in different epochs, each exemplifying the virtues and spiritual path laid down by Shri Guru Dattatreya. Their lives and deeds serve as an extension of Shri Guru's legacy, inspiring countless devotees to walk the path of righteousness, compassion, and spiritual awakening. The first of these revered incarnations is Shripad Shri Vallabh, whose life marks a significant chapter in the history of the Datta Sampradaya.

SHRIPAD SHRI VALLABH

Shripad Shri Vallabh is recognized as the first prominent incarnation of Shri Guru Dattatreya within the revered tradition of the Datta Sampradaya. His earthly existence is dated to the 14th century, specifically spanning the years 1320 to 1351. He was born in the sacred town of Peethapuram, located in the present-day state of Andhra Pradesh, India.

According to an esteemed legend associated with his family, Shripad Shri Vallabh's grandparents undertook a profound and elaborate Yadnya, a ritual of sacred fire. At its culmination, Lord Ganesh is believed to have manifested in a divine form to accept the Purnahuti—the final and most significant offering of the ritual. During this momentous event, Lord Ganesh assured the family that he would incarnate within their lineage. True to this celestial promise, Shripad Shri Vallabh was born on Ganesh Chaturthi, a day of immense spiritual significance in Hindu tradition.

Displaying extraordinary spiritual inclinations from a tender age, Shripad Shri Vallabh renounced all worldly attachments at the age of sixteen to embrace the austere and devoted life of a Sanyasi. Despite the relatively brief span of his mortal life, his journey was marked by numerous impactful travels across various regions, many of which have become steeped in legends recounting his divine presence and spiritual teachings. These tales endure in the hearts of devotees, serving as an eternal source of inspiration. One of the most significant places associated with Shripad Shri Vallabh is Kuravapura, a site that has ascended to the status of a sacred pilgrimage center for followers of Shri Guru Dattatreya. It was here that his teachings and actions left an indelible mark, establishing Kuravapura as an enduring testament to his spiritual legacy. His profound contributions, rooted in guiding humanity toward righteousness, compassion, and union with the divine, continue to resonate deeply within the Datta Sampradaya tradition.

Shripad Shri Vallabh is believed to have taken Jal Samadhi—a sacred and voluntary conclusion of life—within the waters of the Krishna River. Even after his Jal Samadhi, numerous accounts from his devotees describe visions of him in spiritual form, further reinforcing the belief in his eternal presence.

Shripad Shri Vallabh's life, actions, and spiritual achievements form a foundational chapter in the rich narrative of the Datta Sampradaya. His embodiment of the virtues and teachings laid down by Shri Guru Dattatreya has solidified his role as a timeless beacon of spiritual enlightenment and devotion.

Shripad Shri Vallabh is believed to have taken Jal Samadhi, a sacred and intentional departure from mortal existence, within the waters of the Krishna River. Even after this profound act of spiritual culmination, numerous accounts from his devotees' recount witnessing his presence in a spiritual form. Such experiences have further reinforced the enduring belief in his eternal presence and the continuation of his divine guidance, transcending the boundaries of physical existence.

SHRI NARASIMHA SARASWATI

Shri Narasimha Saraswati is widely regarded as a significant incarnation of Shri Guru Dattatreya, and many believe that he was Shripad Shri Vallabh reborn. According to a revered legend, his mother, in her previous birth, fervently prayed to Shripad Shri Vallabh, seeking a son like him. In response to her devotion, Shripad Shri Vallabh promised that he would be born as her son in her next life.

In this subsequent incarnation, Shri Narasimha Saraswati was born as Narahari to a devout couple, Madhava and Amba Bhavani, who were ardent devotees of Shri Dattatreya. From the very moment of his birth in 1378 in Karanja, Maharashtra, Narahari exhibited extraordinary spiritual inclinations. Unlike ordinary infants who cry at birth, Narahari began his life by uttering the sacred sound of "Omkara," signaling his divine essence and purpose.

His early years were marked by an unparalleled sense of tranquility and spiritual grace. Shri Narasimha Saraswati's presence radiated a profound serenity, and his life unfolded as a testament to the virtues and teachings of Sanatan Dharma, embodying the timeless principles laid down by Shri Guru Dattatreya. His contributions to the preservation and propagation of Sanatan Dharma are celebrated as pivotal moments in the spiritual history of India.

Shri Narasimha Saraswati lived an illustrious life spanning eighty years and his early years were marked with remarkable silence. Until the age of his thread ceremony, he refrained from uttering a single word, causing his parents and neighbors concern that he might be mute or hearing impaired. However, upon undergoing the sacred thread ceremony, Shri Narasimha Saraswati astounded everyone by beginning to recite the Vedas with profound clarity and authority, showcasing his extraordinary spiritual potential. As he grew, Shri Narasimha Saraswati expressed a desire to embark on a pilgrimage to further his spiritual journey. His mother, deeply attached and concerned, requested that he remain at home until she had given birth to more children. Respecting her wishes, Shri Narasimha Saraswati stayed until her request was fulfilled, demonstrating his deep sense of duty and familial devotion. Following this, he embarked on his spiritual journey, which was marked by numerous acts of divine grace and selfless service.

It is said that Shri Narasimha Saraswati waited till his parents had more children, an act reminiscent of Shripad Shri Vallabh who had cured his physically handicapped brothers. His life and teachings have been meticulously chronicled in the revered text known as *Shri Gurucharitra*. This sacred scripture not only details the events of his life but also captures his profound sayings, guidance, and enduring wisdom.

The *Shri Gurucharitra* serves as a timeless beacon of spirituality, recounting the lives and contributions of Shri Dattatreya, Shripad Shri Vallabha, and Shri Narasimha Saraswati. It narrates their immense dedication to preserving Sanatan Dharma while embodying kindness and compassion to all sections of society during turbulent times, fulfilling the spiritual and societal needs of the era.

During his remarkable life, Shri Narasinha Saraswati actively championed the preservation and propagation of Sanatan Dharma, contributing significantly to its values and traditions during a period of considerable upheaval. Historical accounts indicate that Shri Guru extended his divine grace to individuals across various societal strata, including curing the Muslim king of Bidar of a severe ailment. In the revered scripture *Shri Gurucharitra*, Bidar is referred to as Vaidurnagari, highlighting its importance in the narrative of Shri Guru's life and his interactions with the world.

While *Shri Gurucharitra* upholds the traditional virtues and ethical principles of Dharma, it also illustrates Shri Guru's profound compassion and inclusivity. His benevolence extended to all sections of society, transcending social boundaries and caste distinctions. This inclusivity was particularly vital given the turbulent times in which Shri Guru lived, a period marked by significant challenges to societal harmony and spiritual stability. Shri Guru emerged as a beacon of hope and guidance, offering solace and wisdom to those in need while safeguarding the spiritual essence of the era.

Like Shripad Shri Vallabha, Shri Guru's departure was shrouded in divine mystery as he disappeared into a river, an act symbolizing his transcendence beyond the physical realm. However, his celestial presence persisted, as devotees continued to witness his reappearance through acts of divine grace. Shri Guru's life and teachings remain a profound testament to the enduring power of spirituality and the ability to foster unity amidst diversity.

SHRI GURU'S ADVICE

*S*hri *Gurucharitra* serves as a revered scripture chronicling the lives of Shri Dattatreya, Shripad Shri Vallabh, and Shri Narasinha Saraswati, with a significant portion dedicated to the legacy of Shri Narasinha Saraswati. His spiritual journey unfolded across several sacred sites, including Bhilwadi (Audumbar) and Narasobachi Wadi in Maharashtra, as well as Ganagapura in Karnataka, each holding profound importance in the traditions of Sanatan Dharma.

Although *Shri Gurucharitra* strongly advocates for the Brahminical traditions, Shri Guru's guidance and compassion transcended caste distinctions and social hierarchies. Historical accounts within the text highlight his interactions with individuals from various societal strata, demonstrating his inclusive approach to spirituality. People from diverse backgrounds, including those belonging to lower castes, sought Shri Guru's divine counsel and blessings, and he welcomed all with equal grace.

This inclusiveness underscores Shri Guru's commitment to fostering unity and spiritual upliftment during a time of societal turbulence and transformation. His teachings and blessings, which reached across caste barriers, remain a testament to the enduring power of spirituality to unify humanity and offer solace to those in need.

Individuals across various societal strata, including a weaver, a farmer, a laundryman (who was blessed to be reborn as a Muslim king of Bidar), an outcaste, and even a Muslim (a reborn laundryman), were recipients of Shri Guru's divine blessings. Shri Guru Charitra recounts these stories to illustrate the profound inclusivity and compassion that defined Shri Guru's spiritual teachings.

Shri Guru provided extensive guidance on how to conduct oneself in daily life. His teachings were detailed and practical, offering advice on various aspects of personal and spiritual conduct. For instance, he provided instructions on morning routines, including the proper methods for cleaning one's teeth and body. He also addressed situations where water might not be available for purification, demonstrating his adaptability to different circumstances.

In matters of worship, Shri Guru advocated meticulousness, explaining how to perform poojas (rituals), the type of flowers suitable for offering, and the correct approach to consuming food. His counsel was comprehensive and touched upon nearly every aspect of life, from mundane activities to spiritual practices. His focus was on the fulfillment of one's duties and responsibilities rather than the pursuit of elaborate Yogic processes.

Shri Guru's advice extended to women and men alike, with specific guidance tailored for each. His teachings emphasized simplicity, sincerity, honesty, and total devotion as the pillars of a virtuous life. Shri Guru's philosophy encouraged individuals to surrender themselves completely to their duties and trust that divine intervention would follow. Unlike other paths, Shri Guru's way was grounded in practicality and devotion, ensuring that his spiritual guidance could be embraced by all, regardless of their social standing.

Shri Guru emphasized that the fulfillment of one's duties with sincerity and devotion forms the cornerstone of spiritual growth. His teachings align with the principles articulated in the *Bhagavad Gita*, which states, "Whatever you do, do it with total devotion; do not expect anything in return. The fruits will be bestowed upon you in due time." Shri Guru consistently advocated for a life rooted in simplicity, honesty, and surrender, underscoring that such qualities invite divine intervention and support.

Living a humble and ascetic life, Shri Guru remained devoted to spiritual practices near the confluence of rivers. His way of life was marked by minimalism—consuming only what was necessary—and immersing himself deeply in meditation. The establishment of Mathas and other institutionalized practices came later, building upon the foundations laid by his unwavering example of faith and service.

Shri Guru's teachings were carried forward by his principal disciples, who sought to preserve and propagate his wisdom for future generations. The ethical framework he provided emphasized the virtues of simplicity, sincerity, and complete surrender to the divine. In this way, Shri Guru's philosophy continues to inspire devotees, illustrating a path that harmonizes devotion and duty without attachment to outcomes.

SHRI SWAMI SAMARTH

S hri Swami Samarth resided in Akkalkot from 1856
until 1878, marking the final chapter of his earthly
presence. While the exact year and date of his birth
remain unknown, his emergence in Akkalkot is considered
a pivotal moment in the spiritual landscape of the region.
Declaring, "I am Nrusinhabhan, and I have come from
Kardali forest near Shri Shaila," Shri Swami Samartha
connected his identity to the profound lineage of Shri
Narasinha Saraswati, who is revered as an incarnation of
Shri Dattatreya.

As chronicled in sacred lore, Shri Narasinha Saraswati
undertook Jala Samadhi in 1380, a mystical form of entering
water as a spiritual act, disappearing from the human realm.
It is said that his disciples, while preparing a seat of flowers
for him, witnessed him departing in serene transcendence.
What followed was a remarkable tale of penance lasting 300
years, during which he is believed to have remained in deep
meditation, encased within an anthill. Legend holds that a
woodcutter accidentally disturbed him during this period,
yet Shri Guru, demonstrating boundless compassion and
forgiveness, absolved the man of any wrong. Following
this event, Shri Narasinha Saraswati commenced a journey
northward, visiting numerous sacred sites and enriching
the spiritual heritage of the places he traversed.

Shri Swami Samarth, regarded as an extension of this
divine lineage, carried forward the wisdom and teachings of

his predecessors. His wisdom and actions resonated deeply within the spiritual community, leaving an indelible mark that shaped the cultural and religious ethos surrounding Akkalkot and the broader region. His presence, teachings, and unwavering example served as a beacon for devotees seeking spiritual enlightenment, devotion, and guidance in navigating their spiritual paths.

After this, Shri Swami Samarth journeyed to Solapur and resided in the town of Mangalvedha, where he devoted himself to guiding his followers and imparting spiritual wisdom. During this period, it is said that he spent six months at Maniknagar, the sacred abode of Manik Prabhu, who is revered as another partial incarnation of Shri Dattatreya. The two spiritual luminaries were often seen engaged in profound discussions beneath the shade of a tree, exchanging insights on spiritual philosophies and practices.

Shri Swami Samarth's arrival in Akkalkot in 1856 marked a pivotal chapter in his spiritual journey. Shortly thereafter, the year 1857 witnessed the onset of a historic revolt against British colonial rule, commonly referred to as the Indian Rebellion. This uprising was characterized by intense confrontation and widespread bloodshed. Initially, the rebellion saw moments of success; however, it was tragically suppressed with brutal force by the British authorities. Shri Swami Samarth, through subtle gestures and actions, conveyed an indication that the 1857 revolt would ultimately be quelled, reflecting his profound foresight and spiritual perception.

Vasudev Balwant Phadke, a prominent figure who organized another revolt against British colonial rule, sought the blessings of Shri Swami Samarth. However, Shri Swami forewarned him that his efforts would ultimately prove unfruitful, indicating that the appropriate time for such initiatives had not yet arrived. This prophetic insight manifested as reality when Phadke faced betrayal by those he had trained and was subsequently imprisoned, where he tragically passed away in confinement.

Shri Swami Samarth was known to be 'ajanubahu,' an extraordinary physical trait wherein his hands reached his knees while standing—a feature regarded as a mark of distinction among spiritually enlightened beings. Interestingly, Mahatma Gandhi also shared this unique characteristic. Shri Swami's mortal journey concluded in 1878, marking the end of an era rich in spiritual teachings and guidance.

Throughout his lifetime, Shri Swami nurtured and shaped the spiritual paths of numerous disciples, leaving a profound legacy that continues to resonate among devotees across Maharashtra, Karnataka, and Andhra Pradesh. His unwavering devotion was exemplified through his frequent chanting of the name Kartavirya Arjuna, a revered disciple of Shri Dattatreya, thereby reinforcing the divine lineage to which he belonged.

Today, Shri Swami Samarth's teachings and spiritual presence are venerated as an integral part of the cultural and religious fabric of the region. His profound wisdom and foresight, paired with his enduring example of spiritual enlightenment, have cemented his position as one of the most influential spiritual figures in Indian history.

Akkalkot has since become a revered pilgrimage destination, widely regarded as a site imbued with Shri Swami Samarth's spiritual presence. Devotees visiting the town often recount the enduring significance of his comforting assurance: "Do not worry. I am with you." This divine promise continues to offer solace and guidance to countless followers, forming an integral part of the spiritual heritage associated with Shri Swami's life and teachings.

SHRI MANIK PRABHU

I heard about Manik Prabhu from one senior devotee who lived near our house. He had a habit of talking scornfully about almost everyone, but he was reverent towards Manik Prabhu.

Manik Prabhu holds an esteemed position among the spiritual luminaries of India and is widely regarded as a partial incarnation of Shri Dattatreya. His life is a testament to profound spirituality and unwavering devotion, qualities that have inspired generations of followers. Born in 1817 on the auspicious occasion of Datta Jayanti—the day commemorating Shri Dattatreya's birth—His arrival into this world was marked by divine significance. His birthplace, Ladwanti near Basavakalyana in Karnataka, remains a site of reverence for those devoted to the Datta Sampradaya.

Manik Prabhu's legacy is celebrated not only for his spiritual teachings but also for the transformative impact he had on those who came into his presence. His life story, filled with miraculous events and profound encounters, continues to resonate deeply among devotees, enriching the cultural and spiritual fabric of the region.

His parents experienced a divine vision in which Shri Dattatreya revealed that he would be born as their son on the auspicious occasion of Datta Jayanti. This celestial prophecy imparted profound significance to Manik Prabhu's birth.

Manik Prabhu's earthly journey came to an end in 1865 at the age of 47, leaving behind a legacy deeply rooted in spiritual enlightenment. Despite never attending formal education, his childhood was marked by an innate connection to the divine. He often roamed with his friends, engaging in spiritual discovery and performing miracles that left a lasting impression on those around him. His friends recounted numerous instances of supernatural occurrences, further solidifying his revered spiritual presence.

During his formative years, Manik Prabhu often spent extended periods in solitude within the forests. Following the untimely passing of his father, his maternal uncle took responsibility for raising him. However, his uncle's aspirations for Manik Prabhu to engage in worldly pursuits, such as becoming the breadwinner for the family, clashed with the young Prabhu's singular focus on spiritual matters.

The turning point in Manik Prabhu's life occurred when his uncle, frustrated by Prabhu's lack of interest in worldly responsibilities, expressed his displeasure. This confrontation led to a profound transformation. Prabhu left his hometown and sought refuge in a place known as Amrutkund. It was here that an extraordinary event unfolded—Shri Dattatreya himself visited Prabhu and initiated him into the revered Datta Sampradaya. This initiation marked the beginning of a spiritual journey that would inspire generations and establish Manik Prabhu as a luminary within the Datta tradition.

Following this transformative event, Manik Prabhu embarked on a pilgrimage to various sacred sites, deepening his spiritual connection and inspiring the devotees he encountered. During these travels, he composed numerous devotional songs, known as bhajans, which continue to resonate with spiritual seekers today. One notable example is a bhajan written in Marathi during his visit to Pandharpur, titled Manikdas Embraced Shri Vittala, reflecting his profound devotion to the deity.

Prabhu's literary contributions transcended linguistic boundaries. He wrote extensively in Marathi, Kannada, Hindi, Urdu, and Sanskrit, demonstrating his remarkable versatility and ability to connect with people of diverse cultural and linguistic backgrounds. His compositions reflected his inclusive philosophy and served as a bridge between the sacred traditions of different faiths.

Eventually, Manik Prabhu established his residence near Bidar, a location that came to be known as Maniknagar. This settlement grew from a modest collection of huts into a thriving community of followers drawn to his spiritual teachings. The reverence for Prabhu was universal, cutting across religious lines. For the Muslims, he was venerated as a Pir; Lingayats saw him as an incarnation of Shri Basaveshwara; Hindus regarded him as Shri Dattatreya; and Sikhs revered him as Guru Nanak.

Maniknagar became a hub of spiritual activity and a testament to Prabhu's philosophy of unity and inclusiveness. Under his guidance, the population of the settlement grew steadily, fostering an environment where people of different faiths could coexist harmoniously, united by their shared quest for spiritual enlightenment.

The humble hut in which Manik Prabhu resided served as a sanctified space, embodying the essence of the formless divine. Reflecting his inclusive philosophy, this sacred abode welcomed individuals from all walks of life, allowing them to worship and connect with the Supreme Reality according to their own beliefs and traditions. Prabhu firmly upheld the notion that the ultimate truth transcends all religious boundaries and that sincere faith, regardless of its form, leads seekers to their spiritual destination.

Within the flourishing settlement of Maniknagar, Prabhu fostered a unique environment of dialogue and mutual respect. Regular gatherings were held, during which Prabhu engaged with people of varying faiths, answering their inquiries and guiding them with profound wisdom. These assemblies, known as Prabhu's Darbar, symbolized a court not of royalty but of spiritual harmony and intellectual exchange. Renowned musicians often graced these gatherings, performing their art before Prabhu, whose deep understanding of classical music enriched these occasions further.

At the core of Prabhu's teachings lay the philosophy of "Sakalmat Siddhant," which advocated the unity of all faiths under a single divine principle. This doctrine resonated deeply within the community, inspiring a spirit of togetherness and underscoring Prabhu's belief in the universality of spiritual truth. Through these principles, Maniknagar became a living testament to his vision—an enduring beacon of inclusiveness and enlightenment for generations to come.

Manik Prabhu continued to grace his followers with his teachings and blessings until the year 1865. His spiritual influence attracted several revered personalities, including Shri Swami Samarth, Shri Saibaba, and Shri Gondavalekar Maharaj, who visited him and engaged in profound discussions that resonated with the ethos of unity and enlightenment.

Historical accounts suggest that Nanasahib Peshwa, a prominent leader of the 1857 revolt against British rule, sought the blessings of Manik Prabhu. Though unable to meet him personally, the Peshwa sent a representative in his stead. Manik Prabhu provided reassurance, affirming that Nanasahib would be protected and encouraging him to continue his efforts. However, Prabhu, in his wisdom, foresaw that the time for India's independence had not yet arrived.

As his earthly journey approached its conclusion, Manik Prabhu prepared for his final spiritual act—his Sanjeevan Samadhi. He instructed his disciples to construct an underground cell in secrecy, which would serve as his final resting place in a meditative, yogic posture. On November 28, 1865, during Datta Jayanti, Manik Prabhu entered the cell, which was subsequently sealed. The revelation of this sacred event came four days later, marking a poignant moment of reflection and devotion for his followers.

Even today, many believe that Manik Prabhu's presence endures within his Samadhi Mandir, serving as a beacon of spiritual guidance and inspiration. The lineage of his teachings remains unbroken, as he thoughtfully appointed his successor to continue his legacy. The tradition established by Manik Prabhu thrives in Maniknagar, where his philosophy of inclusiveness and divine unity continues to illuminate lives and foster harmony across faiths and communities.

SHRI SAIBABA

In contemporary discussions, Shri Saibaba is often a subject of varying interpretations. There are some who assert that he was a practicing Muslim and should not be venerated alongside the Hindu pantheon of gods, while others believe he was a partial incarnation of Shri Dattatreya. Notably, revered figures such as Shri Swami Samarth of Akkalkot and Manik Prabhu of Maniknagar, both prominently associated with the Datta Sampradaya, have recognized Shri Saibaba as a spiritual brother.

Though his attire and practices indicated his identity as a Muslim mendicant, Shri Saibaba's teachings transcended religious boundaries. He would often greet his followers with the phrase "Allah Malik," emphasizing the universal sovereignty of God. His biography, even stripped of miraculous accounts, remains remarkable and deeply resonant.

Shri Saibaba's journey began when he appeared in Shirdi, a modest village in the Ahmednagar district of Maharashtra. His arrival was met with skepticism due to his attire resembling that of a fakir, which led to him being denied entry into a Hindu temple. Unperturbed, Shri Saibaba found refuge in a deserted mosque, where he eventually made his home. This mosque, devoid of grandeur, became a space of profound spiritual significance.

Throughout his life, Shri Saibaba lived primarily in Shirdi, with few occasions when he ventured beyond the village. Yet, each time he left, he would return to the mosque that he had transformed into a sanctuary of peace and divine connection. His presence gradually drew people from all walks of life, and he became a beacon of spiritual wisdom, fostering harmony between Hindu and Muslim communities. Shri Saibaba's acts of celebrating festivals of both religions—such as lighting lamps during Diwali and observing Ram Navami—symbolized his unwavering commitment to inclusivity and unity.

The legacy of Shri Saibaba continues to inspire followers worldwide, serving as a testament to the boundless nature of spirituality that transcends sectarian divides.

He designated the mosque as 'Dwarka Mai,' drawing a symbolic connection to the Hindu deity Shri Krishna, whose legendary capital was Dwarka in Gujarat. This act mirrored his profound ability to harmonize disparate elements of religious traditions into a unified spiritual vision.

It is said that Shri Saibaba arrived in Shirdi on two separate occasions, but his permanent residence began in 1858. His life was interwoven with mysteries that continue to intrigue devotees to this day. During his early years in Shirdi, he chose to live in solitude, seemingly detached from social interactions. Misunderstood by many at the time, children would often mock him and even throw stones at him. Yet, Shri Saibaba remained unruffled, enduring such acts with remarkable equanimity.

Gradually, his presence began to attract people from diverse backgrounds, drawn to the serenity and wisdom emanating from his persona. Unlike many spiritual leaders, Shri Saibaba did not seek to propagate any new philosophical doctrines or reformist ideas. Instead, his teachings and way of life emphasized the practice of compassion, humility, and devotion, encouraging his followers to pursue a path rooted in universal love and spiritual unity.

As his reputation grew, the enigmatic sage became a beacon of hope and guidance for the villagers of Shirdi and nearby regions. His simplicity, combined with his acts of kindness and wisdom, laid the foundation for the spiritual legacy that continues to inspire millions across the globe. Shri Saibaba's life exemplified the transformative power of quiet resilience and unwavering faith in the ultimate unity of all religions.

Shri Saibaba celebrated both Hindu and Muslim festivals, embodying his inclusive spiritual philosophy. For instance, he lit lamps during Diwali and observed Ram Navami, commemorating the birth of Lord Rama. His devotion transcended boundaries, as he was equally regarded as a devout Hindu and a devout Muslim.

A fascinating anecdote highlights the extent of Shri Saibaba's universal appeal. Once, a Muslim villager approached with a question: "Was Saibaba Hindu or Muslim?" Without awaiting a response, the individual declared their own conclusion: "I believe he was born a Hindu and later adopted Islam because he admired our religion, which I regard as the one true path." Shri Saibaba, however, never engaged in such divisive discussions. His teachings and actions consistently reflected his belief in the ultimate unity of all religions, emphasizing that their spiritual goals converge in the pursuit of truth and salvation. Historical records indicate Shri Saibaba was born in 1838 and departed this mortal world in 1918, living a full and impactful life of eighty years. This span bore witness to his evolution from a solitary, enigmatic sage to a revered spiritual figure whose legacy of harmony continues to inspire devotion across faiths and cultures.

Shri Saibaba's journey from a humble ascetic to a universally revered spiritual figure remains a profound testament to his life's philosophy, which transcended religious boundaries. During his lifetime, his following was modest, comprising mainly villagers from Shirdi and the surrounding areas, along with some influential personalities from Maharashtra who sought his blessings. However, after his demise, Shri Saibaba's fame spread far and wide, and he became renowned across the globe for his teachings and acts of kindness.

At Shirdi, the site where he was interred, his tomb has become a focal point of devotion, adorned with a life-sized idol that is worshipped by countless devotees. This form of idol worship, however, is notable for diverging from Islamic principles, as traditional Islamic teachings do not endorse the worship of idols or tombs. Practices such as venerating dargahs or Mazars are also generally discouraged by orthodox interpretations of Islam. Nevertheless, Shri Saibaba is revered by people of all communities and faiths, illustrating the universal appeal of his teachings.

History is replete with examples of Muslim saints who have seamlessly integrated into Hindu traditions. For instance, Sheikh Muhammad, a Muslim saint, composed abhangas in Marathi extolling Lord Vittala. Similarly, Kabir and Rahim are venerated figures whose spiritual contributions reflect a fusion of Islamic and Hindu thought. Eknath's guru, Chand Bodhala, was also a Muslim, demonstrating that spiritual greatness transcends religious bounds. Shri Saibaba's embodiment of equality and universal brotherhood thus aligns with this rich tradition of inclusivity.

Accounts of Shri Saibaba's life reinforce his saintly character and selfless nature. He perceived all individuals as equals, irrespective of their background, and harbored no worldly desires. If he requested alms or money, it was solely to help others. His humility was further reflected in his daily acts, such as begging for his meals, which underscored his disdain for material possessions. Throughout his life, he lived as a humble fakir and passed away in the same manner, leaving behind an unparalleled legacy.

One of Shri Saibaba's enduring practices was maintaining a sacred fire, known as the Dhuni, which he kept perpetually burning. From this Dhuni, he distributed ash to his followers, believing it to have medicinal and spiritual properties. Additionally, he encouraged his disciples to study and reflect upon the life of Shri Rama, further emphasizing his inclusive approach toward spiritual teachings.

Shri Saibaba's unwavering commitment to simplicity and his dedication to spiritual service underscore his status as a symbol of harmony. His life stands as a powerful reminder that the essence of spirituality lies not in divisive labels but in the universal pursuit of truth and compassion—a principle that continues to inspire generations across faiths and cultures.

MACHHINDRANATH

Machhindranath, also known as Matsyendranath in Sanskrit, is widely regarded as the founder of the Nath tradition, an influential spiritual sect that bridges both Hinduism and Buddhism. His legacy, venerated by followers across diverse faiths, is steeped in mythology and enriched by historical accounts, making him a figure of profound significance in spiritual lore.

Matsyendranath is often associated with the tenth century, though some scholars suggest he may have lived earlier, during the eighth or ninth centuries. Tibetan Buddhist tradition holds him as an incarnation of Lord Avalokiteśvara, underscoring the deep reverence bestowed upon him by multiple spiritual traditions. Legends surrounding Machhindranath abound, each contributing to his mystique and spiritual eminence, with many narratives linking his origins to the sea and the symbolism of fish. One prominent legend recounts how Matsyendranath, as a child, was cast into the waters by his parents, where he was swallowed by a fish. Within the fish, he is said to have spent twelve years, during which he overheard Lord Shiva imparting esoteric yogic secrets to Goddess Parvati. The unborn child, immersed in these sacred teachings, responded to Shiva's discourse, prompting the deity to halt his revelation. Recognizing the child's extraordinary potential, Shiva later brought him forth from the fish and initiated him into the path of yoga, naming him Matsyendranath—'Matsya' meaning fish in Sanskrit. Over time, this name transformed colloquially into Machhindranath, with 'Machhi' reflecting the regional term for fish.

Another tale elaborates on Shiva's promise to guide the child in spiritual practice after his birth. It is said that Shiva instructed the child to seek initiation through Lord Dattatreya and to visit the sacred site of Badrikashrama, where their paths would converge once more. This narrative highlights the divine orchestration of Matsyendranath's spiritual journey and his subsequent rise as a Siddha, a perfected master of yogic wisdom.

The Tibetan tradition further enhances Matsyendranath's profile, considering him an enlightened master whose teachings transcended sectarian boundaries. His contributions to yoga and spirituality are celebrated not only through his practices but also through the enduring Nath lineage, which continues to inspire seekers worldwide. While scholarly interpretations vary on the precise historical timeline of Matsyendranath's life, the recurring motifs in his legends—his association with fish, his miraculous survival within the sea, and his divine initiation—serve to illustrate the universality and richness of his spiritual legacy. His story, woven with symbolism and divine intervention, embodies the transformative power of devotion and enlightenment, standing as a testament to the timeless pursuit of spiritual truth.

Machhindranath's life and teachings represent a harmonious fusion of mythology, historical insight, and metaphysical wisdom. His journey from the depths of the sea to spiritual enlightenment resonates profoundly across cultures and generations, underscoring his role as a revered figure in the realms of both history and spirituality.

Following his extraordinary emergence from the fish and divine blessing, Matsyendranath's life continued to unfold as a remarkable journey of spiritual transformation. According to one tale, he was discovered by a fisherman who brought him forth from the waters. Another legend recounts an incident when Matsyendranath accompanied his father on a fishing expedition. In a profound act of compassion and reverence for life, Matsyendranath released all the caught fish back into the water, defying his father's expectations. This act provoked his father's anger, leading to a moment of discord that ultimately inspired Matsyendranath to leave home and seek solitude in penance.

His spiritual pursuit led him to Badrikashrama, a sacred site where he engaged in intense meditation and ascetic practices. It was here that Lord Dattatreya, a revered figure in spiritual traditions, initiated Matsyendranath into higher yogic wisdom, solidifying his path as a Siddha, a perfected master. While legends enrich the narrative of Matsyendranath's early life, some scholars suggest his origins may be rooted in a fishing community, a theory supported by references in texts such as:

Aadinatho gururyasya gorakashyasya cha to guru|
Matsyasheti varm tamaham vande mahasiddham jagadgurum|

These lines explicitly mention fishing, further hinting at Matsyendranath's ancestral connection to the sea and its symbolism.

Matsyendranath's legacy is steeped not only in mythology but also in profound historical and metaphysical significance, making him an enduring figure of spiritual mastery and universal wisdom. His journey from the depths of the ocean to the heights of enlightenment continues to inspire seekers across cultures and generations.

Matsyendranath, also known as Machhindra, is believed to have lived during the eighth or ninth century, though some scholars, such as R.C. Dhere, have proposed the tenth century as a more plausible timeframe for his existence. His life and legacy are enshrined in numerous stories and traditions, spanning across various regions of India. Many locations associated with him bear his name, adding to the rich tapestry of lore surrounding this eminent spiritual figure.

In the Nath tradition, Matsyendranath is revered as the first Narayan to take human form, a significant figure among the nine Narayanas recognized by this spiritual lineage. His stature as a yogi of extraordinary powers is widely acknowledged. The Nath literature recounts remarkable tales of Matsyendranath's triumphs over notable adversaries, including Hanuman, the legendary warrior and devotee of Rama; Vetal, a formidable warrior linked to Shiva; Kali, the fierce mother goddess; Veerabhadra, a creation of Shiva; and Chamunda, another manifestation of the mother goddess. These accounts not only highlight his unparalleled spiritual and mystical prowess but also underscore the profound debates and intellectual victories he achieved over the devotees and followers of these deities.

Matsyendranath's influence and the stories of his accomplishments continue to resonate deeply within the Nath tradition and other spiritual communities, affirming his role as a beacon of wisdom and an exemplar of yogic mastery.

Matsyendranath is also revered within Buddhist traditions, where he is regarded as an incarnation of Avalokiteshvara. In Nepal, he is worshipped as a Bodhisattva, particularly by the Newar community, who honor his presence through the symbolic representation of a wooden block. This unique form of veneration underscores his spiritual significance across diverse cultural and religious landscapes.

A prominent story recounts Matsyendranath's journey to Kamroopa, a kingdom ruled entirely by women. The queen, Mainavati, was captivated by his charisma and wisdom, leading to their marriage. This marked a significant departure from his ascetic path, as Matsyendranath immersed himself in the life of a householder, seemingly forgetting his identity as a yogi who had renounced worldly attachments. His devotion to his wife became all-consuming, presenting a poignant juxtaposition between spiritual discipline and human affection.

Concerned about this turn of events, Gorakshanath, Matsyendranath's foremost disciple, decided to intervene. Gorakshanath was well aware of the formidable challenges posed by Kamroopa, a kingdom guarded not only by its warrior queen but also by its strict customs. Entry into this realm was nearly impossible, given its exclusive governance by women and its protective measures. The narrative, steeped in mystical elements, reflects the complexities of human relationships and the dynamic interplay between spiritual aspirations and worldly entanglements.

The intricacies of Matsyendranath's journey through Kamroopa continue to resonate in the Nath tradition and beyond, serving as a profound allegory for the delicate balance between renunciation and engagement with the world. This tale enriches his legacy, shedding light on the multifaceted dimensions of his spiritual path and the enduring influence he holds in various religious and cultural contexts.

The kingdom of Kamroopa was not only protected by its formidable queen Mainavati but also under the vigilant guard of the great warrior Hanuman, who ensured its safety day and night. Both Machhindra and Mainavati were aware of Gorakshanath's potential endeavor to reach Machhindra, and an alert was issued throughout the kingdom to caution against his arrival.

Undeterred, Gorakshanath devised a cunning plan to infiltrate this highly protected realm. Disguising himself as a woman, he joined a traveling music ensemble and gained entry into Kamroopa. His mastery of the mridangam, a traditional bass percussion instrument, became his tool of ingenuity. As he performed in the royal court alongside the musicians, the rhythmic beats of his mridangam carried a hidden message: "Chalo Machhindra Gorakh Arya" (Come, Machhindra, Gorakh has come to take you away). This subtle yet powerful signal was meant to awaken Machhindra to the presence of his disciple and remind him of the spiritual path he had forsaken.

Some scholars speculate that Machhindra may have been drawn into the fold of women Tantriks, accomplished Siddhas whose practices followed the esoteric path of Vamachara. This path, though revered for its spiritual attainment, often involved unconventional rituals such as the consumption of wine, mutton, fish, symbolic gestures, and sacred sexual union. These practices contrasted sharply with the ascetic ideals of the Nath tradition, presenting a profound tension between spiritual discipline and the allure of mystical freedom.

The narrative of Gorakshanath's intervention in Kamroopa not only illustrates his unwavering devotion to his guru but also serves as an allegory for the eternal struggle between renunciation and worldly entanglements. It highlights the dynamic interplay of spiritual pursuit and human relationships, enriching the legacy of Matsyendranath with layers of complexity and cultural significance.

The practices referred to as Panch Makaras, stemming from the esoteric traditions of Tantra, are deeply symbolic and derive their names from the initial letter "M." They represent wine, meat, fish, gestures, and sacred union. Gorakhnath, through his profound spiritual influence and unwavering commitment to ascetic principles, succeeded not only in guiding Machhindra away from the allure of Vamachara but also in redirecting the Nath sect as a whole towards the path of renunciation and spiritual discipline. Without his intervention, the sect might have been absorbed into the tantric framework of Vamachara.

Both Hindu and Buddhist traditions link Machhindra with fish and the fishing community, underscoring his widespread cultural and spiritual significance. In Buddhist texts, he is referred to as Minpa or Minanath, while in the Nath tradition, Minanath is described as the son of Machhindra, born to the queen of Kamroopa. This duality of identity enriches the narrative surrounding him, offering varied perspectives on his life and legacy.

In Nepal, Machhindra is venerated as the god of rain, and his legend intertwines with the story of Gorakhnath. It is said that Gorakhnath, in a demonstration of his spiritual power, had withheld the rain-bearing serpents, leading to a drought. When the citizens of Nepal, desperate for rain, beseeched Machhindra for help, Gorakhnath relented and released the serpents, allowing the rains to return. This tale not only highlights the reverence for Machhindra but also illustrates the dynamics between guru and disciple, as well as the interplay between spirituality and natural phenomena.

Machhindra, celebrated as a born Siddha, holds a pivotal place in the origins of Hatha Yoga. He is credited with pioneering its practices and philosophies, laying the foundational framework for this important spiritual discipline. His works, including the Sanskrit text

"Kauladnyannirnaya," delve into Kaul Shaivism and explore the principles of this tantric tradition. Another significant contribution attributed to Machhindra is the "Akula-Viratantra," a seminal text on Hatha Yoga. These writings not only reflect his mastery of esoteric knowledge but also secure his place as a luminary in the realm of spiritual and yogic traditions.

Gorakhnath, Jalandarnath, Kanif Nath, Bhartruhari, Revan Nath, Charpatnath, and Naganath are regarded as the principal disciples of Machhindra. Collectively, they are venerated as the Navanaths, a group of nine sages who play a pivotal role in the Nath tradition, influencing spiritual practices and philosophies across regions.

Temples dedicated to Machhindra are found in various parts of India, including Maharashtra, Madhya Pradesh, and Karnataka, as well as in Nepal. His Jeev Samadhi, signifying his eternal resting place, is located in Sawargaon within the Ahmednagar district of Maharashtra. This site holds great spiritual significance for devotees and practitioners of the Nath sect.

The legacy of Machhindra also extends into literary and cultural narratives. Guru Gobind Singh recounts a story of Machhindra in the revered text, the Dasam Granth, underscoring his significance beyond the bounds of the Nath tradition. Furthermore, stories of Machhindra, especially his ventures in the kingdom of women and Gorakhnath's determined efforts to free him, have become enduring themes in folklore and cinema. These tales have been adapted into numerous films across diverse Indian languages, including Marathi, Hindi, Tamil, and Telugu, spanning from the silent film era to contemporary cinema. Machhindra's influence is not confined to spiritual domains alone; his cultural imprint resonates widely, from temple worship to cinematic representations, illustrating the

profound impact of his teachings and the enduring narrative
of his life across different mediums and traditions.

GORAKSHNATH OR GORAKHNATH

According to the accounts preserved within Nath literature, Matsyendranath, a venerated figure in the Nath tradition, once journeyed to a region known as Chandrapur, situated in Bengal. As was his customary practice, he ventured out seeking alms, following the strict principles of his ascetic life by soliciting raw food at precisely five designated locations.

During his rounds, he encountered a Brahmin woman named Saraswati, who lived with a heavy heart due to her inability to bear children. Moved by her plight, Matsyendranath compassionately offered her sacred ash and advised her to consume it, assuring her that it bore the potential to fulfill her deepest longing for motherhood. However, Saraswati, skeptical of the yogi's mystical promise, discarded the ash into a ditch where cow dung was customarily stored.

Twelve years passed, and the sage Matsyendranath returned to Chandrapur, revisiting Sarasvati's residence. Upon his arrival, he inquired about the son he had foretold would be born to her. Stricken with fear, Saraswati confessed that she had never consumed the ash, revealing instead that she had thrown it away. Concerned for her fate and mindful of the spiritual consequences that might ensue, Matsyendranath requested her to show him the place and she led him to the ditch.

When they arrived at the site, the ditch, now covered with hay, revealed an extraordinary secret. Matsyendranath called out, and to Sarasvati's astonishment, a boy's voice emerged from beneath the layers of cow dung and hay. This child, conceived through the divine potency of the sacred ash, had remained in the ditch for twelve years, awaiting his guru's return and guidance.

This remarkable event underscores the transformative and mystical power attributed to figures like Matsyendranath within the Nath tradition. The boy, later known as Goraksha or Gorakh, would rise from this humble yet extraordinary beginning to become one of the most prominent propagators of the Nath Sampradaya, spreading its teachings and influence across the vast expanse of India.

As the child emerged from the ditch, he was given the name "Goraksha," later known as Gorakh, a title that signifies "protected by the cow," reflecting the mystical circumstances of his origin. Scholars have debated the timeline of Goraksh's life, with Dhere estimating his era to be between 1050 and 1150 A.D., while Dr. Mohan Singh suggests that Gorakh may have been born to a Brahmin widow. In certain texts, such as the Gorakshasidhantsangraha, he is referred to as 'Ishwari Santan,' meaning 'a divine child.' Other accounts, such as the Mahanubhava text Matiratnakar, identify him as a Shudra, while Dhere speculates that he might have been a Kashmiri Pandit.

Gorakh was profoundly learned and adept in various shastras, embodying a vast intellectual and spiritual heritage. His teachings and philosophy transcended regional boundaries, as evidenced by the myriad stories and folklore about him found across India's states. Gorakh's contributions to the Nath Sampradaya were transformative, enabling its principles to reach a wider audience and making its doctrines more accessible to people from diverse backgrounds.

His travels throughout India were instrumental in spreading the Nath Sampradaya, establishing it as a prominent spiritual tradition. Goraksh's influence on the movement is demonstrated by the luminary figures among his disciples, which included Amarnath and Gahininath from Maharashtra, Bhartruhari, a king of Ujjain, Gopichand, a sovereign of Bengal, and Vimaladevi. Through their efforts, his teachings gained further prominence and enriched spiritual discourse across the nation.

Goraksh's pioneering work firmly rooted the Nath tradition in Indian spiritual history, showcasing his vision and revolutionary approach to religious thought and practice.

Gorakhnath's intellectual contributions were vast and encompassed a range of works written in Sanskrit, Hindi, and several regional languages. Among his notable Sanskrit texts are *Amanswa, Amarough, Gorakshashataka, Gorakshagita, Gorakshasamhita, Siddha Siddhant Paddhati,* and *Yogamartanda*. His Hindi compositions are part of the collection known as Gorakshbani, which has been meticulously edited by Pitamber Datt Badathwal.

Gorakhnath was also a staunch advocate for social harmony and religious unity, particularly between Hindus and Muslims. His inclusive vision is exemplified by the presence of Baba Ratan Haji, a Muslim disciple, within his circle. Furthermore, the Rawal branch of the Nath tradition includes several Muslim adherents, reflecting Gorakhnath's efforts to transcend religious boundaries.

Women played a significant role in Gorakhnath's spiritual movement. Among his notable female disciples were Vimladevi and Mayanamati (possibly Mainavati), who were actively involved in the Nath tradition. Additionally, his teachings welcomed individuals from marginalized communities, such as Jalandarnath, who belonged to the Antyaja, a tribal group considered outside the traditional four Varnas.

Through his revolutionary approach, Gorakhnath not only expanded the reach of the Nath cult but also imbued it with a sense of inclusivity and universality that continues to resonate across diverse spiritual and cultural landscapes.

Gorakhnath was undeniably a revolutionary thinker whose ideas transcended the limits of his time. His teachings, rooted in spiritual wisdom, have remained relevant across generations. One of his most significant contributions was the systematization of the Nath cult, which he elevated to a prominent position within the broader cultural and spiritual landscape of India. His efforts not only purified and expanded the cult but also brought it into the mainstream.

Among the many symbolic stories associated with Gorakhnath, one stands out as a testament to his innovative approach and inclusive philosophy. It is the tale of his journey to the kingdom of women, where he liberated his master from the influence of women Tantriks. Far from denoting animosity towards women, this story highlights Gorakhnath's respect for their spiritual capabilities. He recognized their role and welcomed them into the fold of the Nath tradition, ensuring their active participation.

Historical evidence suggests that Gorakhnath lived during the early 11th century, though opinions vary regarding the specifics of his life. It is widely agreed, however, that he was the principal disciple of Machhindranath and instrumental in the purification, expansion, and popularization of the Nath cult. The tradition itself predated Gorakhnath, yet his visionary leadership allowed it to flourish and resonate more broadly.

The exact origins of Gorakhnath remain a topic of debate among scholars. Some argue that he hailed from Punjab, while others contend that he was native to Assam. His remarkable fluency in multiple languages further complicates efforts to pinpoint his geographical roots. Nonetheless, his universal appeal and profound teachings continue to transcend linguistic and regional boundaries, solidifying his legacy as a figure of immense spiritual significance.

Gorakhnath holds a revered position in various spiritual traditions and is mentioned prominently in texts like Guru Granth Sahib and Dnyaneshwari. Kabir, the mystic poet, also makes reference to him, further attesting to his profound spiritual influence. Legendary accounts attribute to Gorakhnath the ability to transcend temporal boundaries, describing him as a Mahayogi and Chiranjeevi—a being who is eternal and timeless.

A notable composition that pays homage to this great sage is the Gorakh Chalisa, a collection of forty verses invoking his divine presence and qualities. The Chalisa is said to have been composed after Tulsidas's celebrated Hanuman Chalisa, signifying its importance in devotional literature. Gorakhnath is regarded as the Supreme Deity in this text, further cementing his role as a central figure in spiritual practices.

Across India, numerous temples and caves are associated with the life and teachings of Gorakhnath, marking places where he is believed to have meditated or imparted wisdom. Among these is the Nath Mandir near the Vajreshwari temple, which is considered his Samadhi site. According to one tradition, Gorakhnath may have originally been a Buddhist before transitioning into Shaivism, reflecting the fluidity and convergence of spiritual philosophies in his era.

Gorakhnath also espoused Advaita philosophy, closely aligning his beliefs with the teachings of Adi Shankaracharya. He advocated for transcending debates between Dvaita and Advaita, emphasizing the unity of all existence rather than dwelling on doctrinal divergences. His inclusive and harmonizing perspective continues to inspire followers across diverse spiritual paths.

Gorakhnath is recognized as one of the foremost pioneers in the tradition of Laya yoga, a profound spiritual practice aimed at achieving the dissolution of the mind into the cosmic essence. His contributions to this field were both groundbreaking and transformative. According to historical accounts, the Gorakpanthi community established free community kitchens, a practice rooted in service and compassion, which continues to operate to this day, demonstrating the enduring legacy of his teachings.

The Gurkhas of Nepal hold Gorakhnath in exceptional reverence, with an entire district in the country named after him—Gorkha District. Local traditions tell of Gorakhnath residing on a small hill in the region, where the inhabitants have constructed a shrine in his honor. His influence is equally prominent in Tamil Nadu, where he is revered as one of the eighteen Siddhars, a group of enlightened individuals within the Tamil spiritual tradition. Known locally as 'Korakkar,' it is believed by some that he took Samadhi in Tamil Nadu, further enriching the state's spiritual heritage. Gorakhnath's literary contributions are vast and significant, encompassing numerous texts that have become foundational to various spiritual disciplines. His efforts to systematize the Nath cult marked a pivotal moment in its history. Gorakhnath's leadership not only elevated the Nath tradition but also played a vital role in steering it away from practices deemed unholy. This reformation paved the way for the emergence of the

Bhakti movement, which subsequently gained powerful momentum and widespread appeal.

Gorakhnath's enduring influence extends beyond the borders of India, encapsulating a universal spiritual ethos that resonates with followers across the globe. Through his transformative work, he gave the Nath cult a refined structure, fostering an environment where devotion and spiritual growth could flourish. His legacy continues to inspire and guide countless seekers on their spiritual journeys, underscoring his position as a luminary in the annals of Indian and global spirituality.

GAHININATH

Gorakhnath, under the guidance of his esteemed guru Matsyendranath, embarked on a significant journey that led them to a village known as Kanakgrama. Here, a transformative event unfolded that would deeply intertwine legend and spiritual heritage.

During their stay, young Gorakhnath encountered a group of village children engrossed in a simple yet creative pastime—they were crafting clay figures, a tradition often associated with the Kumhar (potter) community. Inspired by their activity, Gorakhnath recited sacred mantras imbued with spiritual energy, and through his profound mastery of Siddha practices, he animated one of the clay figures, breathing life into it.

This miraculous act marked the beginning of Gahininath's presence, whose origins are intricately tied to the village and the Kumhar community. The children, overwhelmed by astonishment and fear at witnessing a lifeless clay figure come to life, were struck with awe. According to the Nath tradition, it is said that Karabhanjan Narayana, an exalted spiritual entity, had been awaiting the completion of this clay figure to make his descent into the material world.

Regardless of the mythical aspects surrounding this account, Gahininath's significance transcends folklore. He is revered as an accomplished Siddha, a spiritual adept with extraordinary mastery over yogic disciplines. His emergence not only enriched the Nath tradition but also added depth to its spiritual lineage, further cementing the legacy of Gorakhnath as a luminary within this profound tradition.

The astonished and frightened children hurried to Matsyendranath to recount the extraordinary event they had witnessed—a lifeless clay figure animated by Gorakhnath, which now wept as if infused with a profound spirit. Matsyendranath, with his unparalleled spiritual insight, immediately discerned that the revered Karabhanjan Narayana had descended into the material realm as foretold.

At the behest of Matsyendranath, a Brahmin named Madhu and his wife Ganga assumed responsibility for nurturing and raising Gahininath. This pivotal act underscored Gahininath's roots in the Maharashtrian culture, a fact of significant importance to the lineage of the Nath tradition. Gahininath's spiritual contributions would later become foundational, particularly as he undertook the initiation of Nivruthinath into the Nath cult—a transformative moment in the spiritual history of Maharashtra.

Nivruthinath, in turn, played a vital role in extending the reach of the Nath tradition. He introduced his siblings, including his brother Dnyaneshwar and sister Muktabai, into the cult, fostering the growth of its practices and philosophies. Dnyaneshwar, an iconic figure in Indian spiritual heritage, is best remembered for his monumental work—the translation and elucidation of the Bhagavad Gita into Marathi, accompanied by profound commentaries. This endeavor not only made the sacred text accessible to the Marathi-speaking populace but also laid the foundation for the Vaishnav Bhakti movement.

The Vaishnav Bhakti cult, centered around the worship of Shri Vittala of Pandharpur, achieved immense popularity, becoming a cornerstone of spiritual devotion in Maharashtra. Its prominence, however, eventually overshadowed the Nath tradition, relegating it to a historical and spiritual backdrop. Despite this, the contributions of figures like Gahininath and Gorakhnath remain integral to the spiritual tapestry of India, embodying the timeless pursuit of enlightenment and transcendence.

Gahininath is believed to have lived during the thirteenth century, a period marked by profound spiritual and philosophical developments in Maharashtra. It is within this historical context that Dnyaneshwar and his siblings also emerged, contributing significantly to the spiritual traditions and cultural heritage of the region.

गोरखसुत गहिनी आहे नापसंती बानी|
त्यांनी जानत गुरुपुत सोनी चढे निरबानी

The legacy of Gahininath is distinguished not only by his philosophical contributions but also by the artistic and devotional expressions associated with his name. Numerous songs and Abhangas—devotional verses written in Marathi—are attributed to his spiritual influence. Renowned scholar Pangarkar has documented three Abhangas, reflecting the profound resonance of Gahininath's teachings within the cultural fabric of Maharashtra.

In addition to his compositions, Gahininath's Samadhi, or final resting place, holds significant historical and spiritual importance. Located in Nagar district, this site serves as a revered landmark for devotees seeking to honor his enduring impact on the Nath tradition. The Samadhi stands as a testament to the timeless spiritual heritage that continues to inspire countless seekers on the path of self-realization and transcendence.

आकाश तडतडली मेरु कडाडी|
तरी आत्मसुखगोडी सांगो नये|| ||
ऐसिया निर्धारित जवळी आहे देव|
न धरी संदेह अरे मना||
वायु जरी सुटे ब्रह्मांड हे आटे|
तरी आत्मनिष्ठे भंगलो नेली||

Even if there is turmoil in the sky or explosion in
Meru mountain (a mountain which is supposed to be
at the centre of the earth) one should not talk about
the bliss of self-realization.
One should have firm faith that the God is near us.
Do not have doubt o mind.
Even when there is a stormy wind, or the universe
is coming to an end, the person with strong faith in
one's soul will not break.

The linguistic style and nuanced use of Marathi strongly
suggest Gahininath's cultural and regional identity as
a Marathi individual. He is revered as an incarnation
of Karbhanjan Narayana, a significant spiritual figure.
According to tradition, it is believed that while
Gorakhnath was sculpting a figure out of clay, Karbhanjan
Narayana's essence infused it, symbolizing a profound
connection to divine creativity and spiritual lineage.

Machhindranath entrusted Gahininath to a Brahmin
couple with the instruction that, in due course, Gorakhnath
would come to claim him. It is believed that Gahininath
attained self-realization at the remarkable age of seven, a
testament to his profound spiritual enlightenment.

Over time, the site of Gahininath's Samadhi
was transformed into a Muslim tomb, and caretaking
responsibilities were handed to appointed Muslim priests.
This unique blend of traditions has made the Samadhi

a symbol of interfaith reverence and cultural harmony. Today, it is known as Gaibi Pir and serves as a pilgrimage destination for both Hindus and Muslims, reflecting the inclusive spiritual legacy of Gahininath.

Every year, a grand Jatra is held at this sacred site, drawing devotees and visitors from diverse backgrounds who come to celebrate and honor the enduring spiritual significance of Gahininath's life and teachings.

JALANDARNATH

Shiva, immersed in profound meditation, was destined to be roused in order to bring forth his progeny, the only being capable of vanquishing a formidable demon that threatened harmony and order. The gods deliberated on the means to awaken Shiva, whose wrath was as legendary as his divine powers. It was determined that Madan, the God of Love, would undertake this delicate yet perilous task.

With meticulous effort, Madan invoked Shiva's consciousness, successfully disrupting his meditative state. However, the consequence of this act was swift and devastating. Overcome by fury at the interruption, Shiva unleashed the fire of his third eye, situated on his forehead, and reduced Madan's physical form to ashes. Despite this, Madan did not perish entirely, for gods are eternal and transcend physical existence. Stripped of his corporeal body, Madan came to be known as Ananga, meaning "the bodiless one."

In the aftermath of Shiva's awakening, a profound event unfolded. The energy and essence of Ananga's divine seed began to manifest within the sacred blaze of the fire. Into this developing entity, Antariksha Narayana infused his spiritual essence, imbuing it with celestial purpose. Meanwhile, King Brihadrava, a monarch yearning for an heir, was engaged in the solemn act of performing a yadnya—a Vedic sacrificial ritual intended to fulfill his heartfelt desire for progeny. Unbeknownst to him, the convergence of divine forces within the fire was about to culminate in an extraordinary revelation.

The priest, deeply immersed in the sacred rituals of the yadnya, discovered a miraculous child emerging from the purifying flames. Recognizing the divine nature of the infant, he presented the child to King Brihadrava, who received this extraordinary gift with profound gratitude and joy. The king, overwhelmed by the fulfillment of his long-standing desire for an heir, bestowed upon the child the name "Jwalandhar," signifying his origin from the fiery pit. Over time, this name evolved into "Jalandhar," marking the boy's celestial beginnings.

Jalandhar, imbued with inherent wisdom and spiritual prowess, displayed the qualities of a Siddha from his very birth. However, the traditions of the Nath cult required every aspirant, regardless of their innate abilities, to undergo initiation under the guidance of a guru. It was Shri Dattatreya, a revered sage and incarnation of the divine trinity—Brahma, Vishnu, and Shiva—who undertook the noble task of mentoring the young Jalandhar. Under Shri Dattatreya's tutelage, Jalandhar honed his spiritual understanding and expanded his divine capabilities.

As time unfolded, Mainavati, the queen mother of Gopichand, herself sought spiritual enlightenment and became a devoted disciple of Jalandhar. Her association with Jalandhar further solidified his position within the Nath cult, highlighting his transformative influence and far-reaching impact on those seeking higher truth and liberation.

Gopichand's wife, Loomavati, harbored strong disapproval of Jalandhar's growing influence and presence within the Nath cult. Driven by her dissatisfaction, she persuaded her husband to eliminate Jalandhar. Succumbing to Loomavati's counsel, Gopichand took the grievous step of burying Jalandhar in a secluded ditch.

However, destiny intervened when Kanifnath, another esteemed figure of the Nath tradition, ventured into Bengal. Upon learning of Gopichand's actions, Kanifnath reprimanded him sternly, compelling the remorseful king to reconsider his deed. Overwhelmed by guilt and seeking redemption, Gopichand unearthed Jalandhar from his burial, acknowledging his error in judgment.

This pivotal moment marked a transformation in Gopichand's spiritual journey, as he too was initiated into the revered Nath cult under the guidance of the enlightened Jalandhar. Consequently, Gopichand dedicated his life to the teachings and propagation of the Nath tradition, leaving behind a legacy of spiritual awakening and profound contributions to the cult's expansion. Further exploration of Gopichand's impactful journey will be elaborated upon in the chapter devoted to his life and teachings.

Jalandharnath is revered under various names across different traditions, reflecting his profound spiritual legacy and cultural significance. In the Nath cult, he is venerated as Jalandharnath, while Tibetan traditions honor him as Jalandharpa. Additionally, he is referred to as Hadipa, a title with intriguing origins. One interpretation suggests that the name Hadipa signifies his birth from a bone of Lord Mahadeva, emphasizing his divine connection. Alternatively, it is posited that he may have belonged to the Hadi tribal community, historically regarded as untouchable, further underscoring his journey of transcendence beyond societal limitations.

In Tibetan lore, Jalandharnath is regarded as the master of Matsyendranath, a pivotal figure in spiritual teachings. Certain Tibetan perspectives identify Jalandharnath with the

Buddhist Siddha Balpad, illustrating his influence extending into Buddhist traditions. There is also speculation that he may have hailed from the city of Jalandhar in Punjab, a connection that adds depth to his identity and historical significance.

The narrative of Jalandharnath is one of remarkable transformation and spiritual attainment. From humble beginnings and a lower caste, he achieved renown as a Siddha, ultimately epitomizing enlightenment and higher truth. His profound teachings and practices, rooted in the Nath tradition, continue to inspire countless seekers across cultures and generations.

There are seven books to his credit, including *Shuddhivajra Pradeep* and *Hevajrasadhana.*

In both the Nath cult and various Buddhist traditions, Jalandhar Nath is honored as a Mahayogi, a title that signifies his extraordinary spiritual accomplishments and unwavering dedication to the path of enlightenment. Within these traditions, he is also regarded as a direct disciple of Lord Shiva, further underscoring the profundity of his teachings and practices.

One of his notable contributions to the discipline of Hatha Yoga is the technique known as "Jalandhar Bandha." This yogic action, which involves pulling in the naval area while holding one's breath, is believed to have been introduced by Jalandharnath himself. It stands as a testament to his innovative approach to spiritual practices and his enduring influence on the field of yoga.

KANIF NATH

Kanif Nath, celebrated as a devoted disciple of Jalandhar Nath, holds a distinguished place in spiritual lore. Born to King Surath and Queen Bhamini, the royal rulers of Bhadra Loka, his birth was considered a divine blessing bestowed upon his parents by Jalandhar Nath himself. The royal couple fervently prayed for a son who would guide them and their subjects toward salvation, a wish that was fulfilled when Jalandhar Nath intervened and initiated Kanif Nath into the path of spiritual enlightenment.

Kanif Nath's unwavering devotion to his guru is reflected in his relentless quest to rejoin Jalandhar Nath after his initiation. During his search, he stumbled upon a startling revelation: King Gopichand, in an unfortunate turn of events, had buried Jalandhar Nath beneath a heap of dung. Demonstrating remarkable courage and determination, Kanif Nath either freed his revered master himself or compelled King Gopichand to perform the task, thus restoring Jalandarnath's dignity and presence.

Despite being born into wealth and privilege, Kanif Nath chose to renounce all worldly luxuries in pursuit of eternal truth. His profound dedication to the spiritual path led him to wander alongside his guru, embracing an ascetic life that resonated with the principles of selflessness and enlightenment. Kanif Nath remains an emblem of spiritual perseverance, inspiring countless seekers to transcend material desires and strive for higher realms of understanding.

Kanif Nath's Samadhi is located in Nivadunge, approximately 43 kilometers from Ahmednagar, Maharashtra. Revered by locals who affectionately refer to him as Kanhoba, the Samadhi temple stands atop a hill, offering a serene and spiritually enriching environment. At the temple's entrance, one can find the sacred Paduka—traditional footwear—of Matsyendnath, an esteemed figure in Nath tradition. Adjacent to the temple lies a Vitthala temple, dedicated to Vitthala, also known as Kanha, which is another revered name for Lord Krishna.

The annual Jatra, or pilgrimage festival, held at Madhi on Falgun Vadhya Panchami draws devotees from far and wide, many of whom carry wooden sticks as offerings. Among the attendees, the Kaikadi caste, historically categorized as a backward community, forms a significant portion of the devoted pilgrims. A notable tree near Dive Ghat in Pune, perched on a hill of 90 meters, is considered sacred as it is believed to symbolize Kanif Nath's presence. Such sacred sites associated with Kanif Nath can be found scattered across the Indian subcontinent.

Kanif Nath's contributions to spiritual lore extend beyond his physical domains. He is remembered for guiding Goraksha Nath in his search for their mutual guru, Matsyendrnath, revealing that Matsyendra was engaging in worldly pleasures in the kingdom of Kamroopa. Kanif Nath's spiritual journey led him across the Indian subcontinent numerous times, spreading the principles and teachings of the Nath tradition.

His influence reached even the royal courts, as demonstrated by his connection to Chhatrapati Shivaji's daughter-in-law, Yesubai. During a critical juncture in history, Yesubai, the wife of Chhatrapati Sambhaji, prayed to Kanif Nath for the protection of her son, Shahu, who had been imprisoned under house arrest by Emperor Aurangzeb. This display of faith highlights Kanif Nath's reputation as a figure of divine intervention and unwavering spiritual wisdom.

Following Shahu's release, the significance of Kanif Nath's Samadhi grew substantially, drawing devoted followers and expanding its spiritual influence. Shahu generously donated the lands at Nivadunge and Madhi to Gangaram Dikshit for the upkeep of the Kanif Temple, thereby ensuring its preservation and continued reverence.

Kanif Nath is believed to have been a contemporary of Gorakhnath, placing his existence around the eleventh century. His legacy transcends religious boundaries, as he is venerated by individuals across both Hindu and Muslim communities. Kanif Nath's teachings and spiritual endeavors gave rise to his own Shakti-centric cult known as Wamrig, which emphasized the worship of divine feminine energy. Notable adherents of this cult include Siddha Shrungeri, often referred to as Gopichand, a significant figure who carried forward the Wamrig tradition.

The Seplas, a community of snake charmers and traders in venom, trace their origins to the Wamrig cult, as do the Kanifpanthi Yogis. These Yogis, who are known for their ascetic lifestyle, long locks, and expertise in handling snakes, hold Gorakhnath in high esteem as their spiritual guide. Kanifpanthis are characterized by their practice of begging and their dedication to the Nath spiritual lineage. An intriguing legend associated with Kanif Nath highlights his distinct relationship with Gorakhnath. When Gorakhnath invited his disciples to express their desires, Kanif Nath requested a cup of venom, symbolizing his unique spiritual perspective and unwavering commitment to transcend worldly constraints. This act of seeking venom signifies the profound mysticism and resilience that underpins Kanif Nath's teachings and the broader Nath tradition.

Kanif Nath's request for a cup of venom, granted by his Guru, symbolized his profound spiritual commitment and unique approach to transcendence. This gesture, far from being mere symbolism, laid the foundation for the Kanifpanthi community's deep connection with snakes, as protectors and handlers. Among these are the Kalbelias from Rajasthan, renowned as snake catchers, charmers, and traders in venom, whose traditions align with the spiritual lineage traced to Kanif Nath.

In Buddhist tradition, Kanif Nath is referred to as Kanpa, celebrated as a Mahayogi within Vajrayana Buddhism in regions such as Tibet and Nepal. One account portrays him as an initially arrogant monk who, after being initiated into Hevajra Sadhana by Jalandarnath, attained extraordinary yogic powers. These powers, however, led to a confrontation with an equally formidable woman, whose curse is believed to have caused his demise. Another narrative suggests that Kanif Nath voluntarily entered Samadhi, retreating into an underground cell that remains closed to this day.

In Bengal, Kanif Nath is venerated under the name Kanhupa and is regarded as one of the Siddhacharyas, spiritual teachers who composed devotional couplets in early Bangla. Twelve dohas, or two-line verses, are traditionally attributed to Kanhupa, reflecting his profound spiritual insights and contributions to devotional literature.

During Jalandarnath's absence, Kanif Nath played a pivotal role in maintaining the order established by his predecessor, ensuring the continuity of their spiritual practices. Kanif Nath's legacy is immortalized in his Samadhi

Mandir located in Madhi, in the Ahmednagar district, a site of great reverence and pilgrimage to devotees who honor his teachings and contributions.

Kanif Nath's enduring influence as both a spiritual teacher and cultural figure spans geographical and religious boundaries, showcasing his profound impact on diverse traditions and communities.

BHARTRUHARINATH

Bhartruhari, renowned as both a monarch and a philosopher, was the legendary king of Ujjain. Historical accounts often associate him as the sibling of Chandragupta II, also known as the celebrated Vikramaditya. The king's life was intertwined with tales of wisdom, valor, and profound moments that shaped his legacy.

On one occasion, Bhartruhari embarked on a hunting expedition, venturing into the dense wilderness that echoed with the vitality of nature. Amidst the verdant landscape, his eyes fell upon a magnificent sight—a herd of deer, their movements graceful and synchronized, led by a commanding figure, a tall and majestic antler. The regal presence of the antler was unlike any other, embodying strength and responsibility as it shepherded its herd through the forest.

He was about to kill him when his wife Pingala said, "Please, do not kill him, this stag is the husband of 1700 deer. He takes care of the whole herd. If you kill him, you kill 1700 deer."

The king did not listen to her and killed the stag with his lance.

Surprisingly, the dying stag spoke in a human voice, "You have killed me for no reason. I have not offended you. Now, at least fulfil my death wish."

"Please allocate my horns to Shingibaba. My eyes should be given to a woman in need of stability. My legs may be provided to someone who has lost their way, and my ashes should be entrusted to a ruler with a burdened conscience." The king was moved. Even at the moment of death, the stag was still thinking of helping those in need.

He carried the dead stag on his shoulders and proceeded back.

On the way, he met Gorakhnath.

He prostrated before the powerful Nath and requested that he bring the dead stag back to life.

Gorakshnath agreed on one condition.

Bhartruhari had to renounce everything and become his disciple. The stag was revived and returned to its herd. Bhartruhari renounced everything and became a monk.

The tale of King Bhartruhari's transformation into a disciple of Gorakhnath is steeped in spiritual intrigue and profound philosophical undertones. The incident involving the antler marked a pivotal moment, initiating Bhartruhari's renunciation of worldly life. Some suggest this was orchestrated to bring him into the Nath tradition, a spiritual sect devoted to yogic practices and enlightenment.

Another narrative revolves around the king's deep love for his wife, which was later marred by suspicion and doubt, prompting him to abandon the trappings of royal life. Yet another version recounts the heartbreaking loss of his beloved wife, which left him disillusioned with worldly pleasures and inspired his spiritual awakening. Despite variations in these stories, one common thread persists: Bhartruharinath, once a ruler who embraced the luxuries and joys of marital life, ultimately forsook it all to walk the path of asceticism as a follower of Gorakhnath.

To this day, traces of his legacy remain interwoven in the cultural and spiritual fabric of the region surrounding

Ujjain. One notable location is the cave on the banks of the Kshipra River, known locally as the Shipra River, which bears the name 'Bhartruhari Gumpha.' It stands as a silent witness to his journey from monarchy to monasticism and continues to inspire seekers in their quest for higher truths. There are many stories about him in and around Ujjain.

There are three books to his credit.

1. Neeti Shatak,which tells about morals.
2. Vairagya Shatak talks about renunciation.
3. Shrungar Shatak talks about love.

The third book, which explores themes of love, might have been composed during Bhartruhari's youthful days when romantic inspiration was at its peak. Conversely, the first two books, focusing on morals and renunciation, are likely products of his later years, reflecting a more mature and philosophical outlook.

Notably, all three works share the common feature of containing precisely one hundred verses, a hallmark of his literary style and poetic discipline. Bhartruhari demonstrated remarkable prowess as a poet, effortlessly employing a wide array of literary devices to craft his compositions. His works have garnered admiration and remain significant contributions to Indian literature.

Historical accounts add layers of intrigue to his persona. A Chinese traveler is said to have described Bhartruhari as a Buddhist monk, though scholars speculate this may refer to a different individual altogether. Regardless of the specifics, Bhartruhari's legacy is marked by his multifaceted excellence—be it as a ruler who was known for his effective administration, as a devoted husband deeply in love with his wife, or later as a spiritual ascetic advocating the practices of the Nath sect.

As a poet, Bhartruhari's mastery is reflected in the composition of his three celebrated works, collectively known as the 'Shatakas,' as well as his significant contributions to the field of grammar through Vakpadiyam. His ability to embrace and excel in each role he undertook illustrates a life lived with purpose and passion, leaving a legacy that continues to inspire scholars, poets, and spiritual seekers alike.

This suggests that Bhartruhari was not only a celebrated poet and philosopher but also a significant figure in the field of grammar. His scholarly contributions, particularly through the composition of Vakpadiyam, underscore his intellectual versatility and profound mastery of language.

However, some historians and scholars propose that the author of Vakpadiyam might have been a different individual, possibly the Bhartruhari referred to by the Chinese traveler in the seventh century. This ambiguity adds an intriguing layer to the historical narrative surrounding Bhartruhari's legacy.

Furthermore, textual analysis and historical evidence place Bhartruharinatha in the 11th century, offering a distinction between these two figures and their respective contributions to literature, philosophy, and spiritual traditions.

CHARPATNATH

The narrative surrounding Charpatnath is steeped in mythology and symbolic interpretations, reflecting both divine origins and his significant role within the Nath tradition.

According to one tale, during the auspicious occasion of Parvati's marriage, Brahma, overcome by celestial beauty, inadvertently allowed his seed to fall upon the earth. Seeking to conceal it, he attempted to step on the fallen essence, which subsequently divided into two distinct parts. From one arose Balkhilya, a venerable sage, and from the other emerged Charpatnath. The infant was discovered by Satyashrawa and Chandra, who nurtured him and raised him as their own. These caretakers were members of the Chaaran caste, a community renowned for their poetic prowess in glorifying monarchs and composing laudatory ballads for royal courts. Such tales of divine parentage may have been woven into Charpatnath's story to elevate his stature and sanctify his legacy.

An additional symbolic account suggests that Charpatnath was the spiritual progeny of Gorakshanath, the esteemed founder of the Nath sect. This allegorical connection is particularly intriguing, as Gorakshanath, being a revered ascetic, was devoid of earthly desires, including sensuality. This interpretation reinforces Charpatnath's initiation into the Nath tradition under the guidance of

Gorakshanath, further solidifying his esteemed position as a spiritual disciple and adherent of this profound lineage.

Historical analysis places Charpatnath in the eleventh century, aligning his presence and contributions with the flourishing era of Nath philosophy and spiritual practices. This timeline is corroborated by his initiation by Gorakshanath, highlighting his integration into the rich tapestry of Indian spiritual traditions.

Such narratives not only illuminate Charpatnath's divine and philosophical significance but also underscore his pivotal role in shaping the cultural, poetic, and spiritual heritage of his time.

In Tibetan tradition he was the guru of Minpa and is called Minchetsat.

Charpatnath was also a great poet and his songs are meaningful.

They provide tuition for students of Yoga.

इक सेति पाच,,इक निली पटा
इक तिलक नेऊ, लांबी जटा
इक पीए इक कनिफट
जब आवैगी कालि घटा

He talks about the different cults and comments that the outward formalities do not matter.

In another song,

.चरपट आहे दुनियाका भेद
ते क्यु पाऴ ये क्यु देव
पुंगी पण साठा सब जग नाठा
जोत सरुपी संग्रही तांडा तारका भ्रम ना वीरा
मन नहीं मुंडे केस
केस मुंडा था कैसा उपदेश
बोले चरपट तत्वज्ञान

There are a number of books in Charpatnath's name. They are:

1. *Charpatshatak*
2. *Charpatshabdi*
3. *Charpatrasayan*
4. *Charpatpanjari*

One of these four, *Charpatrasayana* is on chemistry.

Charpatnath was indeed a multifaceted person who had an interest in many branches of knowledge.

CHOURANGI NATH

Chourangi Nath, a notable disciple of Matsyendranath, is renowned for his extraordinary transformation and spiritual journey. His tragic story begins with his life as a Prince, the son of King Devpal. Due to the malicious scheming of his stepmother, Chourangi endured a grave punishment when his hands and legs were severed—a fate imposed by his father, who was deceived by false accusations.

तो मत्स्येंद्र सप्तश्रृंगी|. भग्नावयवा चौरंगी |
भेटला की तो सर्वांगी|. संपूर्ण जाला ||

Matsyedra saw Chourangi on Saptashrngi with cut limbs.
When he met Chorangi he got his limbs back.

He is also known as Sarangdhar and Puran Bhagat.
In Nath cult and Buddhist tradition he is regarded as Mahayogi or Mahasiddha.
According to Leela Charitra and Dnyaneshwari, Chourangi's hands and legs were cut on Saptshrungi, or he might have been cured there.
Matsyendranath discovered Chourangi during his travels and, recognizing his potential despite his tragic circumstances, restored him to a state of wholeness.

This miraculous revival, as noted in various traditions, transformed Chourangi's life and led to his revered status within the Nath cult and Buddhist tradition.

Chourangi's imagery and idols often depict him with an additional pair of hands and legs, symbolizing his transcendence beyond physical limitations. These representations also hint at the possibility that, despite being physically challenged, he might have utilized a low wooden seat, known as a "chouranga," to aid his mobility. This detail provides a fascinating explanation for the additional pairs of limbs depicted in his iconography.

Through his resilience and spiritual evolution, Chourangi not only overcame his physical challenges but also became a beacon of inspiration and devotion, embodying the transformative power of faith and yogic practices.

NAGNATH

There are two stories, and possibly two Nagnaths. Some people even believe that the Nagesh cult does not have any connection to the Naths at all. However, the stories are enlightening.

Nagnath, revered as one of the Nine Nathas, holds a significant place in the spiritual landscape of Maharashtra. His principal center is located in

Vadval, also known as Vadvalsiddha Nagesh. According to ancient lore, his origin is intertwined with the mystic elements of Brahma's creation. It is said that a cobra swallowed Brahmadeva's seed, and Agnihotra Narayana subsequently entered the womb. The cobra later laid an egg, from which the child emerged when the time was deemed auspicious. The infant was discovered in the hollow of a banyan tree.

A Brahmin named Josh Sharma happened to pass through the area and, upon hearing the cry of the baby, took it into his care and brought it home. Owing to his unique birth in the hollow of a banyan tree, the child was named Vadval Siddha Nagesh, more commonly known as Nagnath. His foundational contributions to the spiritual tradition led to the establishment of the Nagesh Sampradaya, a branch of the Nath sect, with Vadval serving as its primary hub. This location lies approximately 25 kilometers from Latur, making it an accessible site of pilgrimage for devotees.

Nagnath's work primarily centered on Maharashtra, where he emerged as a beacon of spiritual guidance and transformation. His legacy continues to inspire generations, as his teachings remain a cornerstone of the Nath sect's practices and philosophies.

According to one revered legend, a young boy who was an ardent devotee of Nagnath called upon him with unwavering faith. In response, Nagnath manifested before the boy in the form of sacred Lingas, symbolizing divine presence and spiritual power. This extraordinary event is believed to have taken place in Narendrapura, a location that is today known as Narande in the Kolhapur district.

The boy, identified as Adnyan Siddha, later rose to prominence for his deep spiritual wisdom and literary contributions. He authored numerous significant texts that continue to enrich the spiritual discourse within the Nath tradition. Adnyan Siddha ultimately attained Samadhi in Narande, further sanctifying the site and rendering it a focal point of devotion and pilgrimage.

To honor his legacy and the miraculous encounter, an annual Jatra is held at Narande, drawing thousands of pilgrims and devotees who gather to pay tribute and partake in the spiritual festivities. This event not only commemorates the profound connection between Adnyan Siddha and Nagnath but also serves as a reminder of the enduring spiritual heritage that continues to inspire generations.

REVAN NATH

Revan Nath is revered as an incarnation of Chamas Narayan, born from the seed of Brahma. His extraordinary story begins with a farmer named Sahajsarukh who discovered the infant on the banks of the sacred Reva River. Naming the child Revan Nath, the farmer unknowingly set the stage for a life of profound spiritual significance. Revan Nath later received initiation and blessings from Shri Dattatreya, marking the beginning of his spiritual journey. His physical form ultimately attained Samadhi at Renavi, a village near Vita, which has since become a site of immense spiritual importance.

The narrative of Revan Nath's awakening is both compelling and transformative. In his early years, Revan Nath remained unaware of his divine nature and lived a humble life as a farmer. One day, as he hurriedly worked in his fields, Shri Dattatreya appeared before him, radiating divine presence. When Shri Guru touched Revan Nath, he experienced an immediate realization of his inner self and his extraordinary destiny as one of the Narayanas. Filled with gratitude, Revan Nath prostrated before Shri Guru and humbly requested his blessings. Shri Guru, recognizing the latent spiritual potential within Revan Nath, awakened his consciousness and imparted sacred knowledge that would transform his life forever.

After Shri Guru departed, Revan Nath began to recall the mantras taught to him and meditated upon them with unwavering focus. During his work in the fields, he invoked one of the mantras, and the goddess associated with that mantra appeared before him in divine glory. She granted him an extraordinary boon, telling him that whatever he desired would manifest. With selfless intent, Revan Nath asked for immense wealth, not for personal gain, but to help alleviate the suffering of others.

This pivotal moment marked the beginning of Revan Nath's philanthropic journey. Blessed with vast riches, he dedicated himself to serving the people of his village and beyond. He provided food, clothing, and other necessities to those in need. His ability to heal the sick and resolve the problems of the villagers further solidified his reputation as a spiritual and compassionate figure. Over time, he became known as 'Revansiddha,' a name that symbolizes his divine connection and wisdom.

Revansiddha's legacy of selfless service and spiritual wisdom continues to inspire countless devotees. His life offers profound lessons on the importance of humility, awakening, and the power of faith in transforming lives and communities. Today, his Samadhi remains a sacred place of pilgrimage, attracting those seeking solace, guidance, and spiritual enrichment.

Overwhelmed with his newfound wealth, Revan assured his father that their worries were now a thing of the past. He revealed the abundance of gold filling their chambers, leaving his father astonished yet grateful. From that day forward, Revan embarked on a mission of generosity, dedicating himself to the welfare of the people in his village and beyond. He provided food, clothing, and other necessities to anyone in need, solidifying his reputation as a beacon of compassion and selflessness.

In addition to his material contributions, Revan demonstrated extraordinary capabilities in healing the sick and addressing the difficulties faced by the villagers. His profound wisdom and unwavering dedication to their well-being earned him the revered title of 'Revansiddha,' symbolizing his spiritual enlightenment and divine grace. One day, the esteemed sage Macchindranath arrived in the village of Bund Hal. Hearing tales of Revansiddha's unparalleled kindness and miraculous deeds, Macchindranath was intrigued and sought to learn more about this extraordinary individual from the villagers. Their accounts painted a vivid picture of Revan's transformation into a figure of immense spiritual significance and set the stage for a fateful encounter between the two enlightened souls.

Upon consulting with the villagers, Macchindranath concluded that Revan was one of the Narayanas, a figure of remarkable spiritual significance. The following day, Macchindranath demonstrated his profound compassion by feeding the animals of the village, an act that drew creatures from all corners to partake in his offerings. Witnessing this extraordinary event, Revan felt inspired to replicate such a virtuous deed.

Determined to achieve the same spiritual eminence, Revan invoked the goddess with sincere and fervent prayers. To his astonishment, the goddess appeared before him, her presence radiant and awe-inspiring. She explained that such acts of universal compassion and service were reserved for realized souls who had attained divine grace. She then advised Revan to seek the blessings and guidance of Shri Guru, an enlightened spiritual master, to further his journey toward realization.

Moved by her words, Revan embarked on a pilgrimage to the sacred site where he had first encountered Shri

Dattatreya, a revered figure in his spiritual awakening. There, he devoted himself wholeheartedly to penance, immersing himself so deeply in prayer and meditation that he became oblivious to all worldly distractions. His unwavering dedication marked a pivotal moment in his transformation, one that would soon lead him toward greater spiritual enlightenment and purpose.

Revan's father grew increasingly concerned as Revan neglected his health and even refrained from eating while immersed in his spiritual endeavors. Desperate to aid his son, he sought the counsel of Macchindranath, explaining the severity of Revan's condition. Moved by the father's plea, Macchindranath extended his own efforts and turned to Shri Guru, a revered spiritual figure, for assistance.

In response to Macchindranath's earnest request, Shri Guru manifested before Revan, breaking through the boy's unwavering concentration. Shri Guru, recognizing Revan's immense potential and dedication, welcomed him into the Nath cult's profound spiritual tradition. Thus, Revan was initiated and bestowed with the title of Revan Nath, symbolizing his transformation into a realized spiritual master.

Revan Nath embarked on a remarkable journey across India, dedicating himself to spreading the teachings and philosophy of the Nath cult. His travels were marked by humility, wisdom, and the intent to enlighten countless seekers yearning for spiritual guidance. As with many luminaries of the Nath tradition, Revan Nath contributed significantly to the literary heritage of the cult. Though his compositions were numerous, they have regrettably been lost to time, leaving only his legacy and influence as testimony to his profound contributions.

Among adherents of the Nath cult, Revan Nath is regarded with immense reverence. It is a common belief among followers that invoking his blessings prior to embarking on an endeavor ensures its successful completion.

This tradition underscores the enduring faith in his spiritual power and benevolence.

The final resting place of Revan Nath is located in Vita, situated in Sangli District, Maharashtra. The site of his Samadhi continues to attract devotees and pilgrims, who visit to pay homage and seek blessings, further solidifying his indelible mark on the spiritual landscape of India.

ADBANGINATH

Adbanginath's story is a captivating narrative steeped in spiritual significance. Originally a humble farmer named Manik, his journey into the Nath cult began with a seemingly ordinary act of kindness. One day, Gorakhnath, a revered figure in the Nath tradition, passed by Manik's farm while enduring the pangs of hunger and thirst. Moved by his plight, Manik offered food and water, demonstrating compassion and generosity.

Deeply touched by Manik's gesture, Gorakhnath expressed his gratitude by declaring, "Son, ask for anything, and I shall grant it to you." However, Manik, with a hearty laugh, replied, "When you cannot provide for your own needs, how can you offer me anything?" This response impressed Gorakhnath immensely, as he recognized Manik's wisdom and inherent spiritual awareness, qualities that marked him as a potential Siddha.

Realizing Manik's exceptional potential, Gorakhnath smiled and proposed a unique vow, asking Manik to promise that henceforth he would abstain from pursuing personal desires and refrain from acting purely upon his own wishes. Manik, intrigued and respectful, agreed to the terms. This promise would become a foundational aspect of his spiritual journey, symbolizing his dedication to a higher calling.

True to his pledge, Manik demonstrated astonishing resolve. Upon completing his daily farm work, he refrained from returning home, choosing instead to honor his promise by standing motionless in contemplation. Recognizing the depth of Manik's commitment and spiritual discipline, Gorakhnath shared this remarkable story with Machhindra, another esteemed figure in the Nath tradition, who was eager to witness the farmer's profound spiritual transformation firsthand.

Thus began the evolution of Manik into Adbanginath, an enlightened soul whose journey continues to inspire adherents of the Nath cult and seekers of spiritual truth. His story exemplifies the virtues of humility, selflessness, and unwavering devotion to a path of higher realization. It is a testament to how ordinary acts can lead to extraordinary spiritual awakening, leaving an indelible mark on the legacy of the Nath tradition.

Manik's interactions with Gorakhnath were marked by a candid and unorthodox demeanor. When Gorakhnath approached him and posed a series of questions, Manik's responses were sharp and unconventional, earning him the unique name "Adbanginath." This name, reflective of his distinct personality, became synonymous with his identity as he embarked on his spiritual journey.

Recognizing Manik's latent potential and unconventional wisdom, Gorakhnath proposed a pivotal transformation. He asked, "Will you be my master?" To this, Manik responded with surprise and humility, saying, "You be my guru." With this profound exchange, Gorakhnath initiated Manik into the Nath tradition by uttering the sacred mantra, thereby heralding the emergence of Adbanginath—a figure destined to leave a lasting legacy within the Nath sect. Adbanginath's initiation was remarkable not just for the formalities but for the essence it carried. His rough language and distinct manner of expression further distinguished him, embedding his identity deeply within the spiritual fabric of the Nath cult. His Samadhi, a sanctified resting place, is located in Dudulgaon near Alandi in Maharashtra, serving as a site of reverence and inspiration for followers. There is also another location associated with Adbanginath's intense penance, underscoring his spiritual discipline and commitment.

Adbanginath's narrative bears striking parallels to that of Adbhutananda, an esteemed disciple of Shri Ramkrishna. Adbhutananda, who began his journey as a devoted servant to Shri Ramkrishna, attained enlightenment through his master's constant guidance and presence. His transformation into Swami Adbhutananda exemplifies the profound impact of spiritual mentorship—a theme resonating deeply within Adbanginath's story.

The life of Adbanginath stands as a testament to the transformative power of spiritual dedication, humility, and unwavering adherence to a higher path. His journey continues to inspire seekers of truth, highlighting that even the most unassuming individuals can ascend to extraordinary spiritual heights.

THE NATH TRADITION

The Naths existed as a spiritual group even before the era of Matsyendranath, who is traditionally revered as the founder of the Nath sect, and his prominent disciple Gorakhnath. Prior to their formal establishment, Naths were broadly recognized as Yogis or Jogis, a term encapsulating all practitioners of Hatha Yoga.

The designation "Yogi" is inclusive, applying to anyone dedicated to the disciplined practice of Hatha Yoga. Within their ranks, there are ascetic monks who embrace celibacy and renounce worldly possessions. Characteristically, these wandering sadhus traverse the land, sustaining their livelihood through alms. When visiting households, they invoke the sacred phrase "Allakh Niranjan," and in return, are offered grains or flour by the householders—provisions they prepare themselves.

In contrast, a substantial number of Naths are householders, leading family lives while adhering to their spiritual practices. Despite their divergent lifestyles, these Yogis share a unified commitment to the pursuit of self-realisation. Their presence is widespread across India and Nepal, forming a diverse and inclusive community.

Naths transcend caste boundaries, drawing adherents from various social strata. Some disciples hail from Kshatriya and Brahmin communities, while others belong to lower castes, emphasizing the sect's egalitarian ethos. Notably, the Nath tradition also includes Muslim disciples, reflecting its openness and integration of diverse cultural and religious backgrounds.

This inclusivity and adaptability have allowed the Naths to flourish as a spiritual movement, bridging communities and fostering unity through their profound emphasis on self-realisation, discipline, and devotion. Their legacy continues to inspire spiritual seekers, offering profound insights into the universality of human experience and the transformative power of spiritual practice.

The Nath tradition is notable for its inclusivity and harmony with diverse religious practices. Naths maintained amicable relations with several other spiritual groups such as Vaishnavas, Shaivas, Veershaivas, Buddhists, Mahanubhavas, and Sufi saints. This openness allowed some Naths to attain esteemed positions within Buddhist traditions, and others to be revered as Pirs among Muslims. For instance, Jan Pir is identified as Jalandarnath and Gaibi Pir as Gahininath. The Samadhi sites of several Naths bear a resemblance to the tombs of Muslim saints, symbolizing an interfaith dialogue deeply rooted in their practices. Furthermore, elements of Muslim culture are discernible in their devotional songs, underscoring their adaptability and integration.

Primarily regarded as Shaivas, the Naths trace their origins to Aadinath, one of the appellations of Lord Shiva. Their philosophy emphasizes self-realization and spiritual discipline, chiefly achieved through the rigorous practices of Hatha Yoga. Matsyendranath, also known as Machhindranath, is celebrated as the first human guru of the Nath Sampradaya, laying the foundational principles and spiritual framework of this venerable tradition.

The Nath's commitment to transcend religious boundaries and foster unity has been instrumental in shaping their legacy. Their teachings continue to inspire a diverse range of spiritual seekers, nurturing a profound respect for the universality of human experience and the transformative power of spirituality. With their ability to build bridges across cultures, the Nath tradition remains a testament to the enduring value of inclusivity and mutual understanding in the quest for self-realization and enlightenment.

The Nath tradition reached its full development under the guidance of Gorakshanath, also known as Gorakhnath, the principal disciple of Matsyendranath. Gorakshanath's contributions solidified the spiritual and doctrinal foundations of the Nath Sampradaya, earning him a venerated place within the lineage.

Integral to the Nath's practices is the worship of Shiva, Shakti, and Vishnu. An equally significant figure in their spiritual framework is Shri Dattatreya, regarded as an embodiment of the divine trinity—Brahma, Vishnu, and Mahesh. Shri Dattatreya played a pivotal role in initiating many individuals into the Nath cult, fostering its growth and influence.

Bhairavanath,either, often identified as either one of Shiva's ganas or as an aspect of Shiva Himself, holds a special place within the Nath tradition. This reverence likely stems from the Nath's connection to Tantric practices, which emphasize the interplay of energy and spiritual transformation.

The Nath Sampradaya's doctrinal inclusivity and adaptability have allowed it to harmonize diverse elements, enriching its spiritual tapestry and expanding its influence across regions and cultures.

THE INFLUENCE OF
THE NATH CULT

The Naths have exerted a profound influence across India, leaving their mark on various spiritual traditions and sects, many of which have adopted significant elements from Nath practices. Central to the Nath's philosophy is the veneration of Shiva, a trait that has notably influenced the Lingayat or Veerashaiva communities, who similarly emphasize Shiva worship as a cornerstone of their spiritual identity.

Another notable connection is with the Mahanubhava sect, devoted primarily to Krishna. Despite their distinct focus, references to Nath yogis appear in their literature, illustrating an intersection between these two traditions. A well-documented instance involves Shri Chakradhar, the founder of the Mahanubhava sect, who, upon seeing the attire of a Nath yogi, adopted a similar appearance by smearing ash on his body—a practice characteristic of Nath yogis.

The Naths also deeply impacted medieval Bhakti saints and poets, shaping the devotional landscape of the era. Among the most influential figures is Gahininath, who initiated Nivruttinath, subsequently inspiring his siblings to follow a spiritual path. These saints were accomplished yogis in their own right; however, their adoption of Nath elements focused primarily on the aspect of devotion, or

Bhakti, rather than emulating the external practices and attire of the Nath tradition.

Furthermore, despite the significant reverence these figures held for Nath principles, they did not partake in the pilgrimage practices that were integral to Nath yogis. This selective incorporation reflects the adaptability and enduring appeal of Nath teachings, which continue to resonate across diverse cultures and spiritual frameworks, enriching India's spiritual tapestry in myriad ways.

While these saints revered the Nath principles and incorporated elements of Bhakti into their spiritual practices, they refrained from engaging in the pilgrimage traditions commonly observed by the Nath yogis. This divergence underscores their selective assimilation of Nath teachings, adapting them to suit their devotional focus.

The profound influence of the Naths is also evident in the works of Dnyaneshwar, particularly his magnum opus, the *Bhavarthdeepika,* commonly referred to as *Dnyaneshwari.* This seminal text openly acknowledges the debt owed to Nath philosophy, reflecting the intellectual and spiritual exchange between these traditions.

Furthermore, the Nath yogis extended their reach beyond the boundaries of India, leaving traces in regions now part of Pakistan. Despite the prevailing Islamic faith in these areas, remnants of Nath practices are discernible. For instance, the Rawal branch of the Nath tradition, originating from Rawalpindi, displays unique intersections with local customs. Today, this branch is primarily associated with Pirs and Kalandars, suggesting an enduring influence that transcends religious boundaries.

The Sufi tradition, too, appears to have absorbed certain Nath influences, with some Sufi saints believed to have connections to the Nath lineage. This synthesis between Nath and Sufi elements enriches the tapestry of spiritual traditions in the region, illustrating the adaptability and universality of Nath teachings.

Of particular note is the Nagnath temple in Narande, which intriguingly exhibits architectural features bearing Islamic influences, especially in its outer compound wall. While these elements may have been removed in recent renovations, they serve as a testament to the cultural interplay and mutual respect that characterized the Nath legacy.

The Naths, through their philosophical principles and widespread travels, have left an indelible mark on various spiritual and cultural frameworks, fostering a unique blend of traditions that continues to resonate across generations and geographies.

SOME UNKNOWN TALES
OF THE NATH CULT

The historical narratives surrounding the Nath's often highlight their confrontations with the Shakta tradition, particularly with practitioners of Vamachara. It is widely acknowledged that the founder of the Nath sect, Machhindranath, once succumbed to the allure of a kingdom ruled by women, indulging in a life of sensual pleasures until Gorakhnath intervened to guide him back to the spiritual path. This episode serves as a profound allegory of the triumph of asceticism over worldly temptations.

Another tale recounts a confrontation between a Nath yogi and a female Tantrik, who presented a unique and symbolic challenge. The woman, seeking to assert her tantric prowess, concealed a diamond within her private parts, daring the Nath yogi to retrieve it through intimate union. The yogi, bound by the terms of the challenge, engaged in the act but was unable to emerge, as the Tantrik sought to trap him indefinitely. Ultimately, the Nath yogi succeeded in extricating himself, but his victory came at the cost of the Tantrik's life. This story, though dramatic, is often interpreted metaphorically, illustrating the perils of succumbing to ego and the ultimate transcendence achieved through spiritual discipline.

A different tale speaks of Gorakhnath's encounter with Sohirobanath Ambiye during the latter's journey from Banda to Sawantwadi, carrying a jackfruit in his hand. This meeting is often cited as a pivotal moment in Nath lore, underscoring the sect's emphasis on simple acts of devotion and the transformative power of spiritual initiation.

These narratives serve to enrich our understanding of the Nath tradition, portraying its founders and practitioners as figures navigating complex spiritual and ethical dilemmas. Each story resonates with layers of symbolism, reflecting the Nath's profound influence on the cultural and religious tapestry of the region. Their teachings and practices continue to inspire and adapt across generations, preserving an enduring legacy of philosophical depth and spiritual resilience.

During his encounter with Sohirobanath, Gorakhnath expressed his hunger and asked for something to eat. Sohirobanath, without hesitation, presented the jackfruit he was carrying. Gorakhnath consumed the entirety of the fruit, an act that symbolized spiritual sustenance and acceptance. Following this, he initiated Sohirobanath into the Nath tradition, marking a transformative moment in the latter's life. Sohirobanath went on to compose numerous works in Marathi, including abhangas—devotional songs—that continue to be cherished and sung by devotees to this day.

Another significant episode in Nath history involves the initiation of the Kulkarni siblings. As the four brothers were traveling to Paithan, Gahininath, a respected Nath yogi, appeared before Nivruttinath, the eldest sibling. Recognizing Nivruttinath's potential, Gahininath initiated him into the Nath tradition. This profound spiritual awakening did not end with Nivruttinath; he extended the teachings to his two brothers and sister, thereby weaving the Nath philosophy into the fabric of their familial and spiritual lives. Collectively, the siblings contributed greatly to Marathi devotional literature, composing songs and poems that resonate with themes of devotion, humility, and spiritual enlightenment.

These narratives not only emphasize the transformative power of initiation but also highlight the enduring legacy of the Nath tradition, which blends asceticism with accessible expressions of devotion. Such stories underscore the profound impact of Nath philosophy on regional religious practices and cultural expressions, inspiring generations across linguistic and geographical boundaries.

The Nath tradition underwent significant moderation when it embraced the principles of Bhakti Yoga. This particular form of yoga emphasizes the chanting of the Lord's name as a primary act of devotion, known as Namsmarana in Marathi or Sumiran in Hindi. Unlike ascetic practices, Bhakti Yoga encourages followers to remain engaged in their worldly responsibilities while simultaneously dedicating their minds and hearts to the divine. Its flexibility and accessibility have made it an enduring aspect of devotional practices.

Central to this Bhakti movement is Shri Vitthala, whose venerated temple is situated in Pandharpur, Maharashtra. Devotees undertake pilgrimages to Pandharpur twice annually, embodying the spirit of unity and devotion. The first pilgrimage occurs during the month of Ashadha, according to the Hindu lunar calendar. This sacred journey, known as Wari, draws people from diverse castes, communities, and regions, who come together to walk hundreds of miles from their villages to the temple of Shri Vitthala.

The culmination of this pilgrimage aligns with the eleventh day of the first fortnight of Ashadha. Along the route, villagers provide the pilgrims with food, shelter, and unwavering support, turning the journey into a collective celebration of faith and solidarity. This ritual demonstrates the profound integration of spiritual devotion within the lives of ordinary people, transcending barriers of caste and color to foster a shared expression of reverence.

The tradition of Wari is not limited to the Ashadha month. It is observed again during the Kartik month of the Hindu calendar, ensuring that the cycle of devotion continues to resonate throughout the year. Such practices highlight the inclusivity and enduring appeal of Bhakti Yoga, bridging the gap between rigorous asceticism and accessible spirituality through community and shared devotion.

The tradition of Wari is observed not only during the Ashadha month but also in the Kartik month of the Hindu calendar, ensuring a continuous cycle of devotion throughout the year. This practice predates the contributions of Dnyaneshwar, yet it was Dnyaneshwar who infused the Wari with profound elements of Bhakti, elevating its spiritual significance.

Dnyaneshwar is celebrated for his monumental work in translating and interpreting the Bhagavad Gita into Marathi, a text known as the Bhavarthdeepika, or more commonly, the Dnyaneshwari in honor of its author. Far more than a mere translation, this composition stands as an independent and transformative literary masterpiece. For each couplet of the Gita, Dnyaneshwar provides approximately ninety explanatory verses, offering unparalleled depth and clarity to its teachings.

Born to Vitthalpant and Rukmini Kulkarni in 1275 AD in Aapegaon, Dnyaneshwar lived a short yet impactful life of just 21 years. His legacy endures through his writings and the devotion he inspired in countless followers. Tragically, he chose to take samadhi in 1296 at Aalandi, located in Pune district, marking the culmination of his earthly journey.

The familial story of Dnyaneshwar is equally poignant. His father, Vitthalpant, initially renounced worldly life to become a sanyasi without seeking his wife's consent, a decision that was met with societal and spiritual challenges. This act set the stage for a transformative narrative that intertwined devotion, duty, and reconciliation, shaping the lives of those who followed.

Rukmini waited patiently for her husband's return; her days steeped in hope and devotion. As part of her daily routine, she visited the Siddheshwar temple, where she performed circumambulations around a sacred Ajanvriksha, a rare kind of tree, an enduring symbol of her spiritual resolve and devotion—this very tree remains a testament to her faith to this day.

Her unwavering dedication attracted the attention of Ramananda, a revered spiritual teacher, who upon inquiry discovered that her husband, Vitthalpant, who had renounced worldly life to become a sanyasi, had been one of his disciples. Deeply moved by her plight, Ramananda returned to Varanasi and summoned Vitthalpant, urging him to relinquish his sanyasa and resume his worldly duties. Ramananda argued that the act of taking sanyasa without the express consent of one's spouse was both spiritually invalid and ethically untenable. Bound by the guidance of his mentor and the unyielding devotion of his wife, Vitthalpant obeyed and returned to Aalandi, embracing his responsibilities as a household figure.

The couple was subsequently blessed with four children, each of whom left an indelible mark on the spiritual tapestry of the region. Nivrutti, their firstborn, embodied the principle of renunciation. Dnyaneshwar, their second child, was destined to become a beacon of knowledge and wisdom. Sopan, their third child, symbolized the step of progress in the spiritual realm. Finally, Muktabai, their youngest and only daughter, radiated the essence of liberation. Together, these siblings came to represent profound spiritual ideals, elevating their familial story to one of symbolic significance.

At the heart of this narrative lies Vitthal, the presiding deity of Pandharpur, whose presence threads through their lives as a source of divine inspiration and purpose. Their story and its unfolding events continue to resonate as a testament to the interplay of duty, devotion, and spiritual transcendence. Rukmini is traditionally regarded as Vitthal's divine consort, a figure of deep spiritual significance. The names of their children are imbued with profound meanings that reflect their symbolic roles. Nivrutti, their eldest, signifies the principle of renunciation, embodying a life dedicated to spiritual detachment. Dnyaneshwar, the second child, represents the profound pursuit of knowledge and wisdom. Sopan, whose name translates to "step," symbolizes progress and the ascension toward higher spiritual realms.

Finally, Mukta, the youngest and only daughter, epitomizes liberation, the ultimate spiritual goal.

However, the narrative takes a darker turn when the couple faces societal condemnation. According to the legend, Vitthalpant, having taken the vows of a sanyasi, was deemed to have violated sacred norms by reentering worldly life and raising children. This act was seen as a transgression of his spiritual vows, resulting in the family's excommunication. The children, despite their extraordinary qualities, were subjected to ridicule and ostracism, being labeled as the offspring of a sanyasi—a stigma that brought immense hardship upon the family.

The societal wrath bore heavily on Vitthalpant and Rukmini, leading to their tragic demise. Their story unfolds as a poignant reminder of the rigid societal structures of the time and the harsh consequences of deviating from established norms. Yet, even amidst these trials, the extraordinary nature of their children—derided by society—shines through, elevating the tale to one of spiritual resilience and symbolic significance.

The children, often referred to disparagingly as 'Sanyasi's offspring,' faced relentless societal scorn and ostracism. Vitthalpant and Rukmini, overwhelmed by the weight of societal condemnation, sought counsel from the elders within their community. The elders declared that their transgression—a sanyasi renouncing his vows to reenter the worldly life and have children—was an unforgivable sin, warranting a severe penance. Tragically, the punishment decreed was death.

Resolved to uphold the societal order and perhaps seek redemption in the face of unyielding censure, Vitthalpant and Rukmini took the drastic step of ending their lives. They drowned themselves in a nearby pond, leaving their children to fend for themselves in a world that viewed them with disdain.

The plight of the orphaned children, however, transcended mere tragedy. Despite their dire circumstances, the Warkari sect reveres them as manifestations of divinity—incarnations of the Holy Trinity, Brahma, Vishnu, and Mahesh, with Muktabai, the youngest, considered an embodiment of the great Mother Goddess. This spiritual interpretation imbues their story with a sense of profound purpose and celestial significance.

The lives of the Kulkarni siblings were marked by extraordinary events and miraculous occurrences, which continue to hold a revered place in spiritual narratives. Their resilience and divine presence are celebrated in Warkari teachings, not only as symbols of spiritual transcendence but also as reflections of the enduring struggle against The challenges faced by the orphaned Kulkarni children were relentless and deeply poignant. Left to fend for themselves, they often begged for sustenance, relying on the charity of Brahmins who occasionally provided grains, which they would then cook for their meals. Their hardship was so extreme that, as one-story recounts, they were once deprived of firewood to prepare their food. In this desperate moment, Dnyaneshwar, demonstrating extraordinary yogic abilities, heated his own back to cook bread upon it—a testament to his resilience and spiritual prowess.

Life under such conditions was unsustainable. Seeking a resolution, Nivrutti, the eldest sibling, approached respected Brahmins for guidance. He was advised to obtain an official decree from the authorities in Paithan, a city revered as a seat of supreme learning and spiritual authority, equivalent in stature to Kashi. With no means for a bullock cart, the siblings undertook the arduous journey to Paithan on foot, overcoming numerous obstacles along the way.

During this journey, a transformative encounter occurred. Gahininath, a spiritual leader of the Nath sect, appeared before Nivrutti and initiated him into the Nath tradition. This initiation marked a pivotal moment in their lives, as Nivrutti subsequently introduced Dnyaneshwar, Sopandev, and Muktabai to this spiritual path, shaping their philosophical perspectives and writings.

At Paithan, the Kulkarni siblings performed miraculous feats that left a lasting impression on the local community. Dnyaneshwar, in particular, articulated profound philosophical truths, emphasizing the unity of all living beings and the shared experience of pain inflicted upon others. His teachings underscored the interconnectedness of life and the divine essence present within all beings. One notable miracle attributed to him involved inspiring a buffalo to recite Vedic mantras—a symbol of his ability to transcend societal and natural boundaries through spiritual enlightenment.

These events not only served to vindicate the siblings in the eyes of their community but also positioned them as revered figures within spiritual and philosophical narratives. Their journey from societal rejection to spiritual recognition continues to inspire, demonstrating the triumph of resilience, devotion, and profound wisdom over adversity. This might hold symbolic significance. Following their miraculous feats, the authorities in Paithan provided the Kulkarni siblings with the official decree they sought, granting them the recognition required to resolve their hardships.

One particularly intriguing legend recounts the arrival of a yogi named Changdeva, who was rumored to have transcended death and existed for an extraordinary span of 1,400 years. Riding a tiger, Changdeva approached the siblings with great curiosity. The narrative takes a fantastical turn as it describes how the Kulkarni siblings, basking in sunlight upon a wall, are said to have miraculously levitated that very wall toward the approaching yogi. Awestruck by the display of spiritual prowess, Changdeva prostrated himself before the siblings and eventually became a disciple of Muktabai, the youngest of the siblings.

Accounts of the lives of Nivrutti, Dnyaneshwar, Sopan, and Muktabai have been documented by their contemporaries. While these accounts are often interwoven with exaggerations typical of hagiographies, they still provide glimpses into historical truths and the profound impact of their spiritual journey.

One of Dnyaneshwar's most significant contributions to spiritual literature was the creation of the *Dnyaneshwari* or *Bhavarthdeepika*, a Marathi commentary on the *Bhagavad Gita*. According to tradition, Dnyaneshwar dictated this monumental work to Sachidananda at Nevase, seated near a pillar that has since become a site of reverence. Local residents reportedly attended daily lectures as Dnyaneshwar expounded upon the sacred text, enriching minds and spirits alike.

The pillar, located within the temple, remains a revered site for worship among devotees. This sacred pillar stands as an enduring testament to the profound spiritual legacy of Dnyaneshwar, whose contributions to spiritual literature continue to inspire countless individuals.

Dnyaneshwar's *Dnyaneshwari*, a monumental Marathi commentary on the *Bhagavad Gita*, represents a groundbreaking effort to render the sacred teachings of the Gita accessible to the Marathi-speaking populace. This remarkable work features ovis, a poetic meter popularized by Dnyaneshwar, which enriches each couplet of the Gita with profound reflections and annotations. In this text, Dnyaneshwar merged the transcendental philosophy of Vedanta, as established by Shri Shankaracharya, with the devotional fervor of Bhakti, creating a harmonious spiritual synthesis that resonated with the masses.

Despite his revolutionary approach, Dnyaneshwar maintained a tone of respect and forgiveness, even toward those who had once persecuted his family. His philosophy underscored the virtues of compassion and reconciliation, setting an exemplary standard for spiritual leadership.

Beyond the *Dnyaneshwari*, Dnyaneshwar authored several other influential texts that further advanced the ideals of devotion and spiritual enlightenment. His teachings laid the foundation for the Warakari Sampradaya, a Bhakti movement centered around the worship of Shri Vitthala of Pandharpur. This movement, though in existence prior to Dnyaneshwar, was systematized under his guidance and gained widespread prominence due to his efforts.

The Warakari Sampradaya remains vibrant to this day, with devotees undertaking annual pilgrimages to Pandharpur, chanting the names of Dnyaneshwar and other saints as an expression of their unwavering devotion. These pilgrimages symbolize the enduring impact of Dnyaneshwar's teachings and their ability to transcend barriers of caste and time.

Dnyaneshwar's untimely passing at the age of twenty-one, marked by his voluntary Samadhi, was a deeply significant event. His Samadhi, described by the saint Namdeva in what may be regarded as an eyewitness account, continues to be a focal point of reverence and inspiration for followers of the tradition. Similarly, the other Kulkarni siblings also embraced Samadhi, further illustrating the profound spiritual commitment that defined their lives.

Through centuries, the spiritual lineage established by Dnyaneshwar has inspired and nurtured countless saints, who have contributed to the legacy of the Warakari Sampradaya. This movement, characterized by its inclusivity and devotion, serves as a living embodiment of the Nath tradition's influence and the timeless wisdom of Dnyaneshwar.

GORAKHNATH'S BOOKS

Gorakhnath has written numerous books. Some of which are now lost.

Scholars have compiled the following list:

1. *Amanasva*
2. *Amarough*
3. *Prabodh*
4. *Gorakshpaddhati*
5. *Gorakshasamhita*
6. *Yogmartand of 188 shlokas*
7. *Gorakshakalp*
8. *Avadhuta Geeta*
9. *Gorakshageeta*

Several works listed are believed to have been attributed to Gorakhnath, although some may have been composed by later Siddhas, reflecting their interpretations of his teachings. Gorakhnath himself emphasized the importance of direct experience and the repeated practice of yoga over adherence to textual authority, advocating a pragmatic approach to spiritual realization.

He championed the idea that the realization of the divine was accessible to all individuals, irrespective of caste, color, or creed—a perspective that was profoundly progressive in its time. Gorakhnath's teachings transcended social and religious boundaries, attracting followers from diverse backgrounds, including Muslim disciples such as Baba Ratan Haji. This inclusivity extended to the Rawal branch of the Nath tradition, which retains Muslim adherents to this day.

Notably, Gorakhnath offered a sympathetic approach toward women, granting them an esteemed position within the spiritual realm. His disciples included accomplished Siddhas such as Vimaladevi and Maimanavati, who were recognized for their spiritual attainments and contributions. Gorakhnath's revolutionary outlook and inclusive philosophy continue to inspire practitioners of yoga and spirituality, reflecting a legacy rooted in universal acceptance and the transformative power of personal discipline.

GORAKSHPADDHATI

Orakshpaddhati stands as an extraordinary treatise, compact in its physical size but vast in its intellectual and spiritual depth. It serves as Gorakhnath's guidance to his followers on the practice of Hatha Yoga, laying out its principles in a straightforward and accessible manner. Within its pages, Gorakhnath emphasizes the importance of disciplined practice as the cornerstone of spiritual development.

The foundational aspect of Hatha Yoga, as detailed in the text, is the practice of asanas (postures). While there exists a multitude of asanas, Gorakhnath particularly extols the virtues of Siddhasana and Padmasana, considering them the most effective for the attainment of spiritual focus. Siddhasana involves folding the right leg so that its heel rests beneath the perineum, specifically at the midpoint between the anus and testicles, while the left leg is positioned atop the genital area. This arrangement can be reversed, allowing for versatility in practice. Gorakhnath highlights these postures as essential for steadying the mind and preparing the body for higher spiritual pursuits.

The text further elaborates on the concept of chakras; the energy centers located within the human body. The first chakra, Muladhara, is situated at the base of the torso and serves as the foundational energy center. Each chakra plays a significant role in maintaining the equilibrium of the body's vital elements and is linked to specific physical and spiritual functions. An imbalance in these chakras can lead to ailments, underscoring the importance of cultivating their balance through focused meditation.

Gorakhnath advises practitioners to approach these practices with utmost caution, highlighting the necessity of guidance from an experienced Guru to ensure both safety and efficacy. Through meditation on the chakras and disciplined practice of asanas, individuals can awaken their spiritual potential and harmonize their inner energies, thus embarking on a transformative journey of self-realization. *Gorakshpaddhati*, therefore, not only serves as a manual for mastering Hatha Yoga but also as a timeless repository of wisdom that continues to illuminate the path for spiritual seekers across generations.

Muladhara is followed by Swadhisthana, which is situated above the genitals. Manipura is located at the naval. Next, Anahata is in the heart, Vishuddha is in throat, and Adnya is between the eyebrows. The final chakra is in the head, where Shiva himself is present.

These chakras are representative of the five fundamental elements—earth, wind, fire, water, and sky— and play a crucial role in sustaining both the physical and spiritual equilibrium within the body. Any disturbance or imbalance in these energy centers can manifest as physical and emotional ailments, emphasizing the importance of cultivating their harmony through disciplined practice and meditation.

To activate and balance these chakras, meditation on each specific energy point is prescribed, but Gorakhnath advises practitioners to exercise utmost caution. The process of awakening chakras requires not only dedication but also the experienced guidance of a Guru to ensure safety and effectiveness. The presence and mentorship of a spiritually accomplished teacher are vital in navigating the intricacies of this transformational process.

Gorakhnath acknowledges that while the activation of chakras can grant the practitioner extraordinary abilities, such powers often pose significant distractions and challenges along the spiritual path. These abilities, though impressive, may hinder the yogi's ultimate goal of self-realization if not approached with humility and restraint.

To further aid spiritual seekers, Gorakhnath introduces various techniques, including specific bandhas (body locks) designed to facilitate the awakening of Kundalini, the dormant energy situated at the base of the spine. These techniques exemplify the tradition's profound understanding of the human body's interconnection with cosmic energy and its capability to transcend earthly limitations.

In this context, historical figures such as Shri Ramakrishna serve as exemplary models. Despite being a naturally gifted Siddha with spontaneous mystical experiences during childhood, Ramakrishna sought the guidance of Totapuri, a renowned spiritual master, during his own spiritual journey. This act of humility and reliance on a teacher underscores the essential nature of mentorship in the pursuit of higher consciousness.

Gorakhnath's teachings, thus, extend beyond the activation of energy centers to encompass the spiritual discipline, ethical conduct, and divine connection necessary for true enlightenment, offering seekers a structured yet profound roadmap to self-realization.

Kundalini, often referred to as the "serpent power," derives its name from its resemblance to a coiled serpent smeared with kumkuma (vermilion). This dormant energy, residing at the base of the spine, holds immense potential for transformation and spiritual awakening. Gorakhnath emphasizes that through rigorous and disciplined practice, particularly the focused application of pranayama techniques, Kundalini can be awakened, initiating its ascent through the chakras.

This energy, revered as the divine power of Shiva or the Mother Goddess, embarks on an upward journey once activated. It sequentially pierces each chakra, gradually moving towards the thousand-petaled lotus known as the Sahasrara Chakra, located at the crown of the head. This final chakra symbolizes the ultimate union with Shiva and represents the culmination of the yogi's spiritual endeavor—reaching the highest plane of consciousness and enlightenment.

However, Gorakhnath cautions practitioners about the extraordinary abilities that may manifest during this transformative process. These siddhis, or supernatural powers, while impressive, can become significant obstacles on the spiritual path if not approached with restraint and humility. The acquisition of such powers may tempt the yogi to deviate from their ultimate goal of self-realization, underscoring the importance of ethical conduct and unwavering focus.

In Gorakhnath's teachings, the awakening of Kundalini is not merely a physical or energetic phenomenon but a profound spiritual practice that demands discipline, guidance, and moral integrity. It serves as a testament to the interconnectedness of the human body and cosmic energy, offering aspirants the opportunity to transcend earthly limitations and achieve divine consciousness.

Thus, within this framework, Gorakhnath presents a structured roadmap to spiritual enlightenment, urging seekers to balance the activation of chakras with the cultivation of virtues and wisdom. This formal approach highlights the transformative nature of Kundalini awakening while underscoring the essential role of mentorship and disciplined practice in navigating this sacred journey.

There are six rules:

1. Aasana
2. Pranayama
3. Pratyahara
4. Dhyan
5. Dharana
6. Samadhi

Every posture derived from the movements of animals is known as an Asana. For instance, the stance of a peacock is referred to as Mayurasana, while the posture of a serpent is termed Bhujangasana. Each Asana serves as a foundational element in harmonizing the body and mind. Following Asana, the practice of controlled breathing, known as Pranayama, is emphasized. This involves a sequence of inhalation, exhalation, and retention, ultimately concluding with exhalation. The discipline of Pranayama is multifaceted and requires the guidance of an experienced expert to ensure its proper execution. Several variations exist within this practice, each catering to different needs and objectives of the practitioner. It is imperative to undertake this under the supervision of a qualified instructor to avoid any adverse effects and to maximize its benefits.

Pratyahara, the withdrawal of senses, constitutes the next discipline. Gorakhnath advocates a mindful approach towards food consumption, recommending that practitioners adopt the principle of "Mitahara," or moderation in eating. Foods that are naturally sweet and rich in water content are deemed ideal for sustaining the body's equilibrium. Overeating is discouraged, as it leads to lethargy and disrupts bodily management. This wisdom, long enshrined in yogic tradition, aligns closely with modern dietary advice, which similarly emphasizes the importance of leaving a portion of the stomach empty to promote vitality and energy.

The fourth rule, Dhyan or meditation, forms the core of the spiritual practice. Meditation is directed towards the chosen deity, or Ishta Devata, as a focal point for concentration and devotion. This introspective exercise enables practitioners to deepen their spiritual connection and achieve a state of inner tranquility.

Through this structured progression, Gorakhnath's teachings provide a comprehensive framework for holistic development, blending physical postures, controlled breathing, sensory management, dietary discipline, and meditative focus. This formalized approach lays a robust foundation for seekers striving to awaken their inner potential and traverse the path of self-realization.

If I believe Ganesh, Hanuman, or any other deity can help, I'll start with that. The names may vary, but there is only one God. Meditation can focus on deities such as Ganesh, Hanuman, or any other divine figure, emphasizing the belief that although names differ, the divine essence remains singular. Practitioners may also meditate on specific points of the body, such as the center of the eyebrows, or on any of the chakras—each representing a focal point of spiritual energy. The second part of Gorakshpaddhati provides detailed guidance on a variety of meditation techniques, making it a valuable resource for those seeking to deepen their practice.

To sustain meditation over time, the practice transitions into Dharana, which involves the firm concentration of the mind. Both meditation (Dhyana) and concentration (Dharana) are challenging disciplines, as the mind is often flooded with distracting thoughts during these practices. Experts recommend either ignoring these thoughts or allowing them to pass naturally, adopting the role of a detached observer. This mental discipline is essential for overcoming disruptions and achieving fruitful Dharana.

The culmination of disciplined practice is Samadhi, the ultimate objective of yogic meditation. Through continuous engagement in Dhyana, Dharana, Pranayama, and Pratyahara, the practitioner awakens the Kundalini—a dormant spiritual energy located at the base of the spine. Once activated, Kundalini ascends through the chakras, ultimately reaching the Brahmarandhra at the crown of the head, where it unites with Shiva, symbolizing the convergence of divine masculine and feminine energies. This union induces a state of deep trance lasting up to twenty-one days.

For individuals with unfulfilled earthly missions, the Kundalini descends back to the Muladhara chakra, restoring the yogi to normalcy. Advanced spiritual teachers, known as gurus, possess the ability to awaken Kundalini in others through techniques such as Shaktipata—a spiritual transmission achieved with just a touch. Historical accounts include Shri Ramakrishna's awakening of Swami Vivekananda's Kundalini, underscoring the transformative power of guru-led guidance.

If the Kundalini does not descend, the yogi attains Moksha, or liberation, marking the cessation of the cycle of life. It is a profound state of spiritual freedom and the ultimate aim of yogic practice. Gorakhnatha also provides various remedies for physical ailments, yet emphasizes respecting the natural functioning of the body, advising against unnecessary disruption of its processes.

This framework underlines the systematic and holistic nature of yogic practice, blending meditation, energy control, spiritual awakening, and physical well-being. It serves as an enduring pathway for those seeking self-realization and inner harmony.

DNYANESHWARI ON KUNDALINI

Dnyaneshwari, authored by the 13th-century Marathi saint-poet Dnyaneshwar, stands as a profound literary and philosophical work rooted in the Bhakti tradition. Dnyaneshwar, also known as Dnyandeva, was a disciple of his elder brother Nivrutinath, who was initiated into the Nath cult by the revered yogic figure Gahininath. While the Nath lineage emphasized yogic practices and renunciation, the brothers—alongside their sister Muktabai—played a pivotal role in harmonizing the principles of Bhakti, or devotional worship, with the spiritual rigor of yogic traditions. This synthesis contributed significantly to the systematization and spread of the Bhakti movement in medieval India.

Dnyaneshwari serves as an expansive commentary on the *Bhagavad Gita*, offering a unique blend of translation and philosophical interpretation. Written in the vernacular Marathi in a poetic form known as "ovi," *Dnyaneshwari* not only elucidates the teachings of the Gita but also incorporates Dnyaneshwar's own insights into the pursuit of self-realization. The *Bhagavad Gita* itself, a sacred dialogue between the divine Shri Krishna and the warrior Arjuna on the battlefield of Kurukshetra, explores diverse paths to spiritual enlightenment and self-realization. *Dnyaneshwari* extends these teachings, making them accessible to a broader audience and providing a detailed critique laden with practical wisdom.

The text highlights various spiritual practices and methods discussed in the Gita, central to achieving self-realization. Shri Krishna's discourse in the Gita outlines paths such as Bhakti Yoga (devotion), Karma Yoga (action), Dnyan Yoga (knowledge), and Dhyana Yoga (meditation), all of which contribute to the liberation of the soul. Dnyaneshwar's commentary elaborates on these paths, delving into their philosophical underpinnings and offering illustrative examples to guide practitioners.

Through its integration of yogic principles and Bhakti devotion, *Dnyaneshwari* has become a cornerstone of Marathi spiritual literature. Its enduring legacy lies in bridging the gap between the esoteric practices of ascetic yogis and the heartfelt devotion of Bhakti practitioners, thereby providing a holistic framework for spiritual growth and self-realization. This masterpiece continues to inspire seekers and scholars alike, serving as an invaluable guide on the journey toward inner enlightenment.

Dnyaneshwari provides an exhaustive explanation of the concepts presented in the *Bhagavad Gita*, delving into each shloka with remarkable depth. For every verse of the Gita, Dnyaneshwar offers numerous "ovis"—a distinct poetic form in Marathi—each brimming with philosophical insights and practical wisdom. Through this meticulous commentary, he enriches the foundational teachings of the Gita, ensuring their accessibility and relevance to seekers. A significant portion of the Gita, particularly the sixth chapter, discusses the practice of Yoga as a path to self-realization. It emphasizes the importance of selecting a serene and conducive environment—a space that is neither excessively elevated nor too low—to begin one's spiritual journey. The text prescribes squatting on a mat made of Kusha grass, symbolizing purity and simplicity, as the ideal posture for meditation.

Dnyaneshwar extends these guidelines with a detailed exposition of yogic practices. He advocates sitting in "Siddhasana," a meditative pose that facilitates physical stability and spiritual focus. Further, he describes the application of "Mulbandha," "Jalandharbandha," and "Udiyanbandha," three essential yogic locks that involve drawing inward the base, navel, and throat, respectively. These practices serve to channel vital energies, enhancing concentration and preparing the aspirant for deeper meditative states.

Finally, Dnyaneshwar underscores the importance of reverence toward one's Guru, urging practitioners to direct their thoughts and devotion to their spiritual guide. This act of surrender not only purifies the mind but also aligns the practitioner with the higher principles embodied by the Guru, serving as a gateway to higher consciousness.

Once the yogic practices are mastered and repeated with dedication, the Kundalini energy is awakened—a transformative force within the practitioner. This awakening is achieved through the disciplined application of pranayama, the artful regulation of breath that encompasses exhaling, inhaling, restraining, and once again exhaling in a measured rhythm.

Dnyaneshwar elaborates extensively on the series of profound changes that occur following the awakening of Kundalini energy, describing each detail with both clarity and depth. While the process may initially appear daunting or even unsettling, it serves as a powerful form of catharsis—a purification that liberates the individual from latent fears and impurities. Through this spiritual cleansing, the practitioner undergoes an extraordinary rebirth, emerging with refined physical and mental attributes and an elevated state of consciousness.

An awakened yogi is often endowed with siddhis, or spiritual powers, which can manifest in various forms such as heightened perception, mastery over natural forces, or even miraculous abilities. However, Dnyaneshwar cautions against becoming entrapped by these powers, as misuse or attachment to siddhis can lead to spiritual downfall. He recounts the tale of a Muslim youth who, under the tutelage of a Siddha, achieved siddhis through rigorous penance. Although initially revered and admired by his community, he succumbed to temptations such as greed and lust, which ultimately led to the loss of his siddhis and left him destitute.

Dnyaneshwar's teachings serve as a reminder that spiritual growth is not merely about acquiring extraordinary abilities but about cultivating humility, purity, and wisdom. Practitioners are encouraged to view siddhis as tools for service and enlightenment rather than symbols of personal glory. This perspective ensures that the aspirant remains aligned with the higher purpose of their spiritual journey. Swami Yogananda, in his renowned work *Autobiography of a Yogi*, offers compelling examples that illustrate the transformative journey of Kundalini awakening and the spiritual challenges associated with siddhis. For those seeking deeper understanding, Dnyaneshwar's teachings provide invaluable insights, particularly in the sixth chapter of the revered text *Dnyaneshwari*. This chapter serves as an essential resource for practitioners and scholars alike, offering extensive elaboration on the nuances and complexities of spiritual awakening.

For those interested, English translations of the *Dnyaneshwari* are readily available, making its wisdom accessible to a broader audience. These translations preserve the essence of Dnyaneshwar's profound discourse, enabling readers from diverse backgrounds to engage with his timeless teachings and incorporate them into their spiritual practices.

THE BHAKTI SAMPRADAYA

The Nath tradition, deeply rooted in the disciplined practice of Yoga, has extensively documented its philosophical and practical teachings through the works of numerous Nath masters. These texts, many of which have been discussed in earlier chapters, serve as foundational guides to understand the interplay between spiritual discipline and enlightenment.

An important aspect to note is the profound influence of the Bhakti movement on the spiritual landscape, which, in many ways, emerged as an extension and evolution of the Nath tradition. The Bhakti cult was championed by saint-poets across India and gained significant traction through the efforts of Shaiva and Vaishnava saints. These luminaries popularized devotion as an accessible and transformative path to spiritual realization, emphasizing that salvation could be attained through heartfelt devotion and unwavering faith in the divine.

The essence of Bhakti lies in its simplicity: devotees are encouraged to chant the name of their chosen deity repeatedly, meditate on the divine form, and surrender their thoughts and actions to God. In this process, the divine is believed to take care of the spiritual and worldly needs of the devotee. What makes the Bhakti movement particularly remarkable is its inclusivity; many of its proponents were householders who demonstrated that spiritual growth does not necessitate renunciation or isolation from daily life.

Their teachings and poetic compositions, often voluminous and profound, continue to inspire millions and highlight the possibility of achieving self-realization within the framework of ordinary existence.

A defining feature of Bhakti poetry is its practical wisdom, aimed at guiding the common man toward spiritual awakening without the need for elaborate rituals or temple visits. Among the numerous luminaries of the Bhakti movement, Kabir stands out as one of the most revered figures, whose contributions left an indelible mark on Indian spirituality.

Kabir, a spiritual luminary of the Bhakti movement, lived and thrived in Varanasi, one of the holiest pilgrimage centers in Hindu tradition, recognized as the dwelling place of Lord Shiva. Despite uncertainties surrounding his parentage, it is widely accepted that Kabir's father was a weaver, a vocation Kabir himself embraced with pride. He never attended formal schooling and often expressed a sense of pride in his unlettered state, asserting that true wisdom transcends academic learning.

An ardent devotee of Lord Rama, Kabir's life, which spanned an extraordinary period of one hundred and twenty years, remains an enduring testament to his spiritual depth and commitment. His timeless couplets, known as *dohas*, continue to resonate with spiritual seekers and the common populace alike, transcending religious and social boundaries. Kabir's message attracted followers from diverse faiths, and his legacy persists through the 'Kabirpanthis,' a devoted community that upholds his teachings and principles.

Legends surrounding Kabir often speak of divine protection, as it is said that Lord Rama and his brother Lakshmana guarded him day and night. This narrative underscores the divine connection that Kabir cultivated throughout his life.

Alongside Kabir, other luminous figures of the Bhakti movement contributed significantly to the spiritual and literary heritage of India. Tulsidas, another celebrated poet-saint, authored the *Ramcharitmanas*, an epic retelling of the Ramayana that remains integral to Hindu devotional practices.

Among these illustrious figures was Meera Bai, a princess and devout follower of Lord Krishna. Born into royalty, Meera Bai was married into the renowned Rana dynasty, which boasts historical figures such as Rana Pratap. Her unwavering devotion to Lord Krishna, despite numerous trials and tribulations, is immortalized in her deeply spiritual hymns and bhajans, which continue to inspire devotees to this day.

Meera Bai endured numerous trials and tribulations in her unwavering devotion to Lord Krishna, yet she never relinquished her faith. Her deeply spiritual hymns, known as bhajans, remain profoundly popular and continue to inspire generations with their heartfelt expressions of divine love. Another notable figure within the Bhakti movement, Namdev, was a contemporary of Dnyaneshwar and is celebrated for his extraordinary spiritual experiences. According to tradition, Namdev is said to have had direct encounters with Lord Vittal of Pandharpur, engaging in daily conversations with the divine. His teachings on Bhaktiyoga, emphasizing devout worship and surrender, were deeply impactful, and his compositions in the form of devotional poetry remain widely sung and cherished to this day.

The Bhakti poets hailed from diverse regions and social backgrounds, contributing richly to the spiritual and literary heritage of India. Each of these luminaries articulated their devotion through poetic compositions that transcended linguistic and cultural boundaries, fostering unity among people of various creeds and castes. This Bhakti movement flourished across the Indian subcontinent, becoming a pivotal cultural force that enriched every major Indian language with timeless devotional literature and inspired countless devotees to seek spiritual fulfillment through unwavering faith and love for the divine.

The Bhakti poets, while acknowledging the significance of yogic experiences, placed greater emphasis on devotion (Bhakti) and the continuous recitation of the divine name as the supreme path to spiritual enlightenment. Among these luminaries, Tukaram emerged as a prominent figure in the 17th century, carrying forward the traditions of the Bhakti movement with profound sincerity and accessibility. Tukaram's life exemplified simplicity and humility, and his poetic contributions, known as abhangas, remain a source of guidance and inspiration for countless devotees. It is believed that his spiritual initiation occurred in a dream, an event that deeply shaped his unwavering commitment to the divine. Many of Tukaram's abhangas are autobiographical in nature, offering intimate glimpses into his personal journey of faith and devotion.

Throughout his life, Tukaram fought tirelessly against superstitions and societal injustices, using his poetry as a medium to challenge dogma and promote spiritual equality. His contributions earned him the revered title of 'Jagadguru,' meaning 'Teacher of the World,' a testament to the universal impact of his teachings and compositions. His legacy continues to enrich the spiritual and cultural fabric of India, inspiring generations to pursue a path of devotion and enlightenment.